Elihu H Shepard

Early History Of St. Louis And Missouri

From It's First Exploration By White Men

Elihu H Shepard

Early History Of St. Louis And Missouri
From It's First Exploration By White Men

ISBN/EAN: 9783741150975

Manufactured in Europe, USA, Canada, Australia, Japa

Cover: Foto ©ninafisch / pixelio.de

Manufactured and distributed by brebook publishing software (www.brebook.com)

Elihu H Shepard

Early History Of St. Louis And Missouri

THE EARLY HISTORY

OF

St. Louis and Missouri

FROM

ITS FIRST EXPLORATION BY WHITE MEN
IN 1673 TO 1843.

BY

ELIHU H. SHEPARD,

FORMERLY

PROFESSOR OF LANGUAGES IN ST. LOUIS COLLEGE.

∗∗∗

SAINT LOUIS:
SOUTHWESTERN BOOK AND PUBLISHING COMPANY,
510 AND 512 WASHINGTON AVENUE.
1870.

PREFACE.

The fortunate withdrawal of the manuscript of the HISTORY OF ST. LOUIS AND MISSOURI from the *Missouri Republican* office but a few hours before its sudden and total destruction by fire, and the more fortunate preservation of the author's AUTOBIOGRAPHY through such a general conflagration, have left it in his power still to expose their contents to the literary world and place them beyond future danger of destruction. Moreover, the advanced age of the author admonishes him to secure his present labors by publishing what he has already finished, and to wait for the rebuilding of the *Missouri Republican* office for completing the later history of the city and the State.

The author hopes this course will be approved by his friends and the public, and, therefore, he adopts it.

Very respectfully,

ELIHU H. SHEPARD.

CONTENTS.

CHAPTER I.

The first Explorations of Missouri by White Men, and the Settlement of Missouri and St. Louis by Pierre Laclede Liguest—The first Mutation in the Government—Arrival of Captain Louis St. Ange de Bellerive and the Troops of the Garrison of Fort Chartres... 9

CHAPTER II.

The first Marriage and first Dedication of a Church in St. Louis—The Death and Burial of the Great Ottawa Indian Chieftain Pontiac and his Dear Friend St. Ange de Bellerive; Both Buried in St. Louis.. 15

CHAPTER III.

The Happy Days of St. Louis and Missouri—The Transfer of the Country from Spain to France, and from France to the United States.. 32

CHAPTER IV.

Raid on Loutre Island by the Indians, and Death of several Prominent Citizens—The Battle of Tippecanoe, and the First Steamboat on the Western Rivers, in 1811—The Great Earthquake and Destruction of New Madrid... 45

CHAPTER V.

Remarkable Performance of Colonel Russell Farnum, a Fur Trader of St. Louis, Missouri... 51

CHAPTER VI.

Reminiscences of Manuel Liza, a Spaniard, and his devotion to the United States in the War of 1812—The first Bank in St. Louis—Duel between Colonel Thomas H. Benton and Charles Lucas, Esq., and the result—The first Brick House in St. Louis—Missouri becomes a State of the Federal Union—The first Iron Foundry in St. Louis.. 55

CHAPTER VII.

The Incorporation of the town of St. Louis by the Legislature, with a Charter for a City—The Expedition of Gen. William H. Ashley to the Rocky Mountains, and his Defeat by Auricaree Indians on the Missouri—Duel between Thos. C. Rector and Joshua Barton, in which the latter was killed.............................. 65

CHAPTER VIII.

The first Female Charitable Society Formed in St. Louis—Return of General Ashley, Successful, from the Rocky Mountains—Election of Hon. Frederick Bates, Governor, and his Early Death....... 70

CHAPTER IX.

The Invitation to the Marquis de Lafayette to Visit St. Louis, and his Acceptance—His Arrival, Reception and Departure........... 76

CHAPTER X.

The Assassination of Mr. Horatio Cozzens—The Seat of Government Removed from St. Charles to Jefferson City—Hon. Thomas H. Benton Re-elected to the Senate of the United States.......... 82

CHAPTER XI.

The St. Louis Arsenal Commenced, and a New Market House on Place d'Armes—Missouri Hibernian Relief Society Organized, and a Colonization Society................................ 87

CHAPTER XII.

The Court House Finished, and an Episcopal Church—The Branch of the Old United States Bank Opened in St. Louis—Inauguration of Water Works System.................................... 92

CHAPTER XIII.

Duel between Hon. Spencer Pettis and Major Thomas Biddle, and the Attending Circumstances..................................... 98

CONTENTS.

CHAPTER XIV.

The Erection of the Second Market in St. Louis, on Broadway—The Sympathy of Missourians with the People of Illinois Distressed by the Black Hawk War—Their Response—Excitement in St. Louis by the Veto of the Bank Bill, July 10th, 1832, by the President—The first Appearance of Cholera............................ 103

CHAPTER XV.

Two Representatives in Congress Elected—The State Enlarged by Act of Congress—How it was Done—Arrival of the Sisters of Charity and Founding of their Hospital—The Legislature Authorizes the Sale of the St. Louis Commons by the City Council, and this enables the Public Schools to commence operations............ 109

CHAPTER XVI.

Rise and Progress of Parochial and other Schools and Colleges...... 115

CHAPTER XVII.

Destruction of the Old Cathedral Building by Fire—The first Railroad Convention in St. Louis—The Murder of Deputy Sheriff Hammond and Burning of the Murderer by the Citizens—The Texan War, in which some Missourians Participated.................. 117

CHAPTER XVIII.

The Appointment of Robert W. Wells to the Bench of the United States District Court of Missouri—The Burning of the first Steam Flouring Mill in the City—Incorporation of the Bank of the State of Missouri—The Overthrow of Rev. Elijah P. Lovejoy's Printing Press by a few Individuals under Cover of Darkness of Night—Organization of General Richard Gentry's Command, their Distant Campaign in Florida, and his Honorable Death in the Arms of Victory... 128

CHAPTER XIX.

Visit of Hon. Daniel Webster to St. Louis—Death of Hon. David Barton, one of the first United States Senators from Missouri.... 135

CHAPTER XX.

The first Public School Houses Erected in St. Louis—Death of Rev. Elijah P. Lovejoy, late of St. Louis, at Alton, Illinois—Burning of the State House and Documents at Jefferson City.............. 139

CHAPTER XXI.

The Ice and Frost of 1838—Opening of the St. Louis Public Schools—Death of Gen. William Clarke, First Governor of the Territory after the Adoption of the Name of Missouri—The Mormons Arrive in Missouri and are Expelled for Misconduct—The Establishment of the St. Louis Criminal Court............................ 145

CHAPTER XXII.

Establishment of the Ten Hour System of Labor—Great Extension of the City Limits and Division into Five Wards—The Abolition of Property Qualifications for Voters—The Murder of Two Young Men by Four Negroes, and their subsequent Arrest, Conviction and Execution.. 151

CHAPTER XXIII.

The Establishment of the Court of Common Pleas—The Appearance of the Native American Party—Death of Hon. John B. C. Lucas. 157

CHAPTER XXIV.

St. Louis Becomes a Manufacturing City—Remarkable Trial of a Circuit Court Judge before a Criminal Court, and his Acquittal—Change in the Manner of Voting in St. Louis County—The Steamer Edna Collapses a Flue and Destroys the Lives of Fifty-five Persons—The Death of Several Prominent Citizens........ 160

CHAPTER XXV.

Remarkable Visit of Audubon, the Ornithologist, to the Mouth of the Yellowstone river, and his safe Return—The Robbery and Murder of Don Chavis on the Santa Fe Road—Visit of Colonel Richard M. Johnson to St. Louis—Death of Major Joshua Pilcher at St. Louis.. 167

HISTORY OF ST. LOUIS AND MISSOURI.

CHAPTER I.

The First Exploration of Missouri by White Men, and the Settlement of St. Louis by Pierre Laclede Liguest—The First Mutation in the Government—Arrival of Capt. Louis St. Ange de Bellerive and Troops of the Garrison of Fort Chartres.

Some of the most pleasing, useful and lasting monuments in history have had their origin in very small and trifling incidents, and are viewed with veneration and delight on account of their artlessness and apparent conformity to everything that surrounds them.

What can be more natural and praiseworthy in the surviving patriarchs and builders of a great city than to leave a history of its date, origin and growth? This subject had long attracted the attention of the old residents of St. Louis, as they saw their older associates who had assisted in building it up in its infancy gradually leaving them, until the last individual was dead, who accompanied Col. Auguste Chouteau to its site and witnessed the first labors for its foundation. A century had nearly elapsed, and more than two hundred thousand people then resided within two miles of the site of the present court house.

The builders of such a city could never let its history perish. More than two hundred and fifty of those who had spent thirty years in its building participated in forming the Missouri Historical Society of St. Louis, at the court house, on the 11th day of August, 1866, being the centenary anniversary of the first grant of land in Missouri.

The same object which induced them to form it has since prompted them to support it, and collect such materials as will enable them by degrees to present a history of the State and of the city which may challenge the scrutinizing view and the austere judgment of the historian on its merit.

We will begin when Missouri was the hereditary domain of the red man, living in scattered bands over this magnificent State, in huts without chimneys, walls, or one stone upon another for protection against enemies or elements.

They obtained their precarious subsistence chiefly by pursuing the inhabitants of the earth and water; had dogs, but no other domestic animals; spoke different languages, and occasionally warred fiercely with each other. Such was its condition when, on the 7th day of July, 1673, a small band of Europeans and Canadians, from Quebec, led by Father Marquette, a monk, and Joliet, a merchant, reached the Mississippi river.

It is evident the red men of Missouri had no hostility or prejudices against strangers, as they allowed them to descend the river to the junction of the Arkansas and to return in peace and publish to the world a description of the most wonderful and mighty river of the world, whether its waters, its length, its magnificence, its branches, or its banks are considered.

Five years later LaSalle, in 1668, navigated the Mississippi to the mouth without meeting with any opposition from the natives dwelling in Missouri, and from that time to the present the aborigines of Missouri have manifested an unusual confidence in strangers from all parts of the world. Hence their country was never made a battle field on which to settle those dreadful controversies which have distracted other sections of our country and filled them with desolation and mourning, while this enjoyed the enviable position of being an asylum.

This state of peace and quietude over the territory now included in the State of Missouri arose from its remoteness from points where the cupidity of wealth had attracted its votaries and kept their attention employed on objects that seemed to promise a more immediate reward.

This continued seventy-three years after LaSalle had explored the Mississippi to the Gulf, until in 1755, when Ste. Genevieve was founded by the French, attracted there by the lead mines in its vicinity, which was the first settlement made by Europeans in the State. There does not appear to have been any purchase made by the original inhabitants at the time, nor does any objection appear to have been made by them to their settlement there or to any of the French settlements made in Missouri, although the Illinois Indians were the acknowledged owners among red men. But in those days the Indian title was not noticed or recognized, as no law had been made to protect them, and they were invaded and their lands appropriated with impunity by those who coveted them.

The peace of Paris, in 1763, made the Mississippi the line between the possessions of France and England. This, however, did not change the Indian title to the country or their intercourse with the French, for the Indians of Missouri continued to trade at the villages of Cahokia and Kaskaskia, until Pierre Laclede Ligueat removed his goods from Fort de Chartres, where he had wintered, to the present site of St. Louis. On the 15th day of February, 1764, his Lieutenant, Auguste Chouteau, the long well-known and much respected Col. Auguste Chouteau, commenced operations on the block next the river, on the south side of Market street, where the Merchants' Exchange now stands, and which had been the site of the only market house which the city contained for about sixty years from its foundation, and gave name to the street on which it was located. Temporary buildings, for the shelter of his workmen and tools, were soon constructed from the timber on the ground, for that part of the city was covered with a growth of the most suitable timbers for that purpose and for the camp fires of the new settlers, so necessary at that inclement season of the year. Early in March Pierre Laclede Ligueat arrived, laid out the plan of the future town, and named it St. Louis, in honor of Louis XV, king of France. In this plan of his city, although he predicted its future greatness, he seems to have overlooked the advantages of broad streets and large blocks, and thereby betrayed his want of knowledge of the liberal scale which has been adopted by all the great builders of beautiful cities in laying out their streets and public grounds.

He, however, manifested a proper respect for religion and sacred things, which is commended at this late day, but which it would then have pained him to have been persuaded that, within one century, it would be so perverted from his design as to quite change its sacred character and nearly obliterate his labor. Having drawn his plan he dedicated the third block from the river, one hundred yards square, adjoining the south line of Market street, to the use of a Catholic church and a cemetery, and it was so used for more than half a century, when nearly every one who had ever seen Pierre Laclede Liguest had been buried in the cemetery.

All those patriarchal remains are now removed and buried under the Cathedral, which, with the Bishop's house, occupies a portion of the south part of the block on Walnut street; the residue is occupied by the most attractive business houses in the heart of the city.

Mr. Liguest was a merchant of no ordinary mind. Others have acquired vastly larger estates than he, but no one has excelled him in pushing forward commercial enterprises in person and planting the seed of a city in more fertile soil and cultivating it with greater success. His scrutinizing eye and sound judgment directed him to the point on the block on Main street directly in front of where the Merchants' Exchange of St. Louis now stands, as being the best place to sell goods on the west side of the Mississippi, in 1764. More than a century has since elapsed and it is the best place yet. On this celebrated block, on which Barnum's Hotel now stands, and on which other stupendous structures unite to cover the whole block, Mr. Liguest erected his dwelling house and store.

When Mr. Liguest had his plans matured to commence the erection of his house, he encountered a peaceful, but most untoward, frightful, annoying and expensive occurrence, that taxed all his patience, prudence, courage, wisdom and perseverance to overcome, but which developed his character and left it to the admiration of posterity. The acknowledged owners, among red men, of all the west bank of the Mississippi, from the Missouri to the mouth of the Ohio, were the Illinois Indians. A village of Missouri Indians, residing beyond this tract, having heard of the advent of the merchant, broke up their winter quarters and came on a begging excursion, to the number of one hundred and fifty warriors, with all their families, outnumbering the Europeans five to one, and in the most confiding, friendly and familiar manner located their huts as near as possible to their new acquaintances, manifesting the utmost pleasure and contentment in their new homes, and exhibiting their willingness to participate in all the labors and enjoyments the place afforded.

It is a remarkable incident, worthy of memory, that the first cellar ever excavated in St. Louis was done by the squaws of this band, and the earth removed to a low place at considerable distance, and payment made for it in beads and other ornaments.

The inconvenience of their presence was soon felt, and their departure requested and refused. They said "they were like the ducks and buzzards, who sought open water to rest and refresh themselves on, and they desired no better place than they now enjoyed."

The prudent Liguest, however, proceeded to no violence against them, but, having supplied them with provisions, he threatened them with the vengeance of the French troops stationed at Fort Chartres, which soon frightened them to a departure in peace. Nor did they ever return or manifest any resentment against him or his people on that account. Being relieved from their presence and confirmed in their friendship, he prosecuted the building of his house and store, enlarged the circuit of the village, and gave encouragement to emigrants, without fear or opposition.

Thus the new colony soon gave evidence of thrift and stability, and stimulated the inhabitants of Illinois, who felt aversion to British rule, to transfer their establishments to the new settlement, which soon changed the current of trade and concentrated it rapidly at St. Louis.

It was in April of this year that M. d'Abbadie, the Commandant General of Louisiana, received orders from his sovereign to proclaim to the people the surrender of all the French possessions west of the Mississippi to Spain.

The people of New Orleans were highly exasperated by the promulgation, and declared they would not be separated from their mother country.

A few months later the intelligence reached St. Louis and

produced the same sensation, and was intensified by the report soon after that M. d'Abbadie, overwhelmed by the orders he had received, had died of grief. This state of public feeling so far manifested itself hostile to Spanish authority that, although the transfer was made in 1762, it was not carried fully into execution until 1769.

A large warehouse was built and occupied on the eastern part of the block which was known as La Place d'Armes at that time, but is now all used for the most extensive mercantile operations.

In the early part of the following summer, 1765, the commandant of Fort Chartres, Louis St. Ange de Bellerive, delivered the possession of the fort to Capt. Sterling, an English officer appointed by his country for that purpose, and removed the garrison of above forty soldiers to the new colony. This added much to its military strength and character, but very little to its moral and industrial habits. The disorder that soon followed demonstrated the necessity of having a governing head to the community, and probably no people were ever blessed with a more suitable or worthy person for a governing chief than St. Ange de Bellerive was for theirs; and their sound judgment and necessity at once assigned him to the place.

He was a favorite with his countrymen, and his name acted as a talisman in securing the respect and affection of the Indians, as they knew him to be an inveterate foe to the English, which was a crowning virtue in *their* eyes. He was the friend of Pontiac, the great chief of the Ottawas and demigod of Western savages.

He alone had been able to persuade Pontiac to bury the hatchet when all his allies had forsaken him. "By their unanimous desire he was vested with the authority of Commandant General, with full power to grant lands and to do all other acts consistent with that office as though he held it by royal authority."

He was the intimate friend of Mr. Liguest, the founder of the town, and like him was never married.

There can be no doubt that Louis St. Ange de Bellerive accepted the authority conferred on him by the people of St. Louis, and acted on it with the approbation of Aubri, the Commandant General of New Orleans, as he was too honorable an officer to administer an authority without the approbation of his superiors. When he had instituted a government, things assumed a more flattering appearance, and several merchants of considerable wealth became residents of the village and built more commodious habitations. Until their advent the house of Liguest, which had the walls of the first story built of stone, while all the other dwellings had their walls built of flattened logs set with one end about two feet in the ground, and the interstices filled with small stones and mortar.

In 1766 St. Ange de Bellerive, having organized his system of government and procured that now venerable and well known book called *Livre Terrien*, commenced making grants of land, hoping for a retrocession of the country to France, when the grants would be legalized by a confirmation.

Two grants were made to Pierre Laclede Liguest on the 11th day of August, 1766—one for the block on which the Barnum Hotel now stands, the other the mill tract on which the old Chouteau stone mill now stands, both of which grants have always been recognized as perfectly legitimate and the most valuable of their size in the State.

CHAPTER II.

The First Marriage and First Dedication of a Church in St. Louis—The Death and Burial of the Great Ottawa Indian Chieftain Pontiac and his Dear Friend St. Ange de Bellerive; Both Buried in St. Louis.

The first marriage in the new colony was celebrated on the 20th of April, 1766, more than two years after its settlement, Toussaint Hanen and Marie Baugenon being the parties to the contract. The first mortgage was recorded as made on the 29th day of September, 1766, by Pierre Berger to Francis Latour, two merchants engaged in the peltry trade; it does not specify any particular article, but pledges all the goods of the mortgagor as security to the mortgagee for the payment of a specified number of bundles of deer skins at a specified time, but without any stipulated value being mentioned in the instrument. It was, however, canceled some years after, by the attorney of the mortgagee acknowledging payment on a simple receipt, attested by a notary and recorded among the archives.

From this transaction we infer there was encouragement given to attorneys at that early day, as well as others, to people the new city, and that payments were as tardy and securities as useful as at the present time. The only exports were furs and peltries, which were currently received as bank notes now are, and their qualities as carefully examined and their values estimated in all transactions.

One year after the grants made to P. Laclede Liguest, when the village had assumed shape and was making a rapid growth under its popular and able magistrate, on the 11th day of August, 1767, the town was thrown into a ferment by the arrival of news from New Orleans of the intention of the Spanish Government to take possession of the country which had been ceded to it under the secret treaty of 1762. This threw a shade over the prospect of the future, and a year of bitter rage disturbed the quiet people of St. Louis, without a foe to fight or means to change their position, when, on the 11th day of August, 1768, a body of Spanish troops, under one Rios, acting under the orders of Don Antonio d'Ulloa, the Governor of Louisiana, arrived and intensified their alarm, but made no demonstrations against the established regulations of St. Ange de Bellerive. Having quietly spent the winter in St. Louis, Rios retired with his small force early in the summer of 1769, to the great relief and joy of the people.

The first season of joy and festivity on their departure had not closed when an event occurred which created a sensation of curiosity to some and pleasure to others, not easily described or ever forgotten by Missouri historians.

It was the arrival of Pontiac, the great Ottawa chieftain, to visit his dear friend and old acquaintance, St. Ange de Bellerive. The fame of Pontiac was as familiar at that time as that of Grant or Sherman at this, from the Mississippi to the Atlantic.

He had formed the confederation of many different tribes of Indians, dwelling hundreds of miles asunder, occupying the district from the Mississippi to the Alleghany, and between the

Ohio and the lakes, to resist the power and encroachment of the English, whom he, as well as most all of the Indians, feared and distrusted more than any other people, and believed, with the assistance of the French, they could drive and confine beyond the Alleghany and Cumberland Mountains. He had won the friendship, confidence and esteem of the chivalrous Montcalm at Quebec; had distinguished himself in the ambuscade and defeat of General Braddock, near Pittsburg; had planned the massacre at Michilimacknac. He had matured the plan and appointed the time for attacking the forts and settlements of the English pioneers, by which more than two thousand of them lost their lives.

These exploits had cast a romance about his name and excited the most intense desire to behold the great chieftain. St. Ange de Bellerive gave him a most cordial reception, corresponding to his former high position, at his own quarters in the house of Madame Chouteau, and he was feted and caressed by many of the principal inhabitants of the village.

The plans of this remarkable chief, although successful and flattering for a time and aided by one of the greatest nations in Europe, had all failed; his allies had all forsaken him; his best friends had persuaded him to bury the tomahawk, and his active mind brooded over his disappointments until he had suffered it to be stupefied by the lethean bowl when out of the influence of his watchful friends. In this state of mind he soon became wearied and restless, and expressed a desire to visit Cahokia, where some French friends had invited him, as he was still the famous Pontiac, and all wished to see him.

His friend, St. Ange de Bellerive, was unable to dissuade him from his purpose. He had fallen. That sublime expression of countenance, which had formerly given evidence of intellect and chivalrous devotion to his country and people, had given place to a bloated visage that betrayed the want of all prudence or self-respect in its present possessor. Still he was the *lion* that attracted all eyes toward him as he went to cross the river to Cahokia in 1769, dressed in a complete uniform which he had received from the unfortunate Montcalm on his visit to Quebec. His friends who remained in St. Louis never saw him alive again. He left with a few followers and arrived at Cahokia, where he drank deeply, until his faculties were stupefied, when he wandered in the underwood about the village where he was tomahawked by a Kaskaskia Indian, who had been hired by an English trader, named Williamson, to kill the great chieftain, for which he was rewarded by the payment of a barrel of whisky. When St. Ange de Bellerive heard that Pontiac was murdered he caused his body to be brought to St. Louis, amid the general mourning of the inhabitants, where it was buried with the honors of war, near the tower which stood at the junction of Fourth and Walnut streets, on the block next south of the Court House, where his remains rested until tradition alone could indicate the spot.

The mighty chief now rested on land owned by those who drank the price of his blood, but who were destined never to visit it again, but to have a place in the history of Missouri in common with him and his avengers; for the great Ottawa chief was too well known and too much beloved by the red warriors of that day to be assassinated and his death go unavenged. The surrounding warriors becoming acquainted with the circumstances of his death, and that the Illinois Indians had drank the price of his blood in a common debauch, their savage instinct was roused, and with a universal howl of vengeance against all who had tasted of the whisky, and the war-whoop still thrilling on their lips, they quickly assembled and assailed the different tribes of Illinois Indians, and nearly annihilated their existence by an indiscriminate slaughter.

: Thus the colonists of Missouri have never been pained by the presence or annoyed by the claims of the Illinois Indians, and the ashes of Pontiac lie in St. Louis, as well as those of his dear friend, St. Ange de Bellerive—repose without a slab or epitaph to mark the spot of their sepulture or to perpetuate their memories. Houses are built where both were buried, and but few know that their remains rest in St. Louis. During the same year, fraught with so many exciting incidents connected with the visit, death, burial and avenging of Pontiac, news came from New Orleans that sent a thrill of terror into the hearts of the inhabitants, and made them tremble in the anticipation of the future. Don Alexander O'Reilly, who had been appointed Commandant General of Louisiana, arrived at New Orleans, with three thousand men to enforce his authority. Seven years had elapsed since France had, without war, ceded the territory to Spain, and several peaceful attempts had been made to obtain quiet possession, without success. In short, a spirit of insubordination had seized the people, and many were assembled to dispute his landing, and were only prevented from attempting resistance by the timely persuasion of the magistrates and principal citizens, when they saw that all attempts to resist such a force would be unavailing.

He landed amid threats and execrations and saw the elements were rife for a spirit of revolt, only waiting a more fitting time to manifest itself more fully. He was not a man to be trifled with or thwarted in the execution of his duties.

He caused twelve of the ringleaders to be arrested, five of whom were shot, one committed suicide, and six were imprisoned in Cuba.

This enabled him to put the Spanish code of laws into operation, which were soon found to be quite as well suited to the taste, and circumstances of the people as those of France.

He then extended the Spanish authority to the Upper Louisiana, by dispatching Lieut.-Gov. Piernas, who arrived in St. Louis in the early part of 1770, and quickly received possession of the country from M. St. Ange de Bellerive. It was with regret and tears the French people saw the flag of their country removed and a foreign banner supply its place.

But with two such men present as Lieut.-Gov. Piernas and M. St. Ange de Bellerive it was not wonderful that such a peaceful and quiet people as the early French colonists were should soon become reconciled, contented and happy in their new condition. In the same year there was a great festival on the occasion of the dedication of the new church, built, according to the custom of the French, with flattened logs set on end in the earth and the interstices filled with mortar, located at the southwest corner of Market and Second streets. The solemn ceremonies were performed on the 24th of June, 1770, being the anniversary of St. John the Baptist, when the inhabitants turned out en masse to worship in a Christian manner the only true God of the universe. The holy Father Gibault, surrounded by his little flock which he had gathered to teach and guide in the fold of the church, said mass, administered the Eucharist and chanted the Te Deum and De Profundis with a heart overflowing with gratitude to the great Benefactor of man.

In performing this duty he must have enjoyed a taste of that ambrosial food which can only be partaken by the holy and the good.

When the benediction had been pronounced and the people dismissed to their homes, there was an universal rejoicing and satisfaction that a church had been completed and the banner of the cross erected in peace; and that their labors received the approbation of Heaven is manifest from the fact that, although a hundred years have since elapsed and every person then present is dead, the worship of God on that block has not been suspended for a single day.

The administration of Don Pedro Piernas, in 1770, commenced under most favorable circumstances for an officer of his kind and liberal disposition, and was conducted with that wisdom and prudence which seldom fail to make both the governor and the governed happy. His predecessor was a most venerable and popular man among a most peaceful people.

They had felt opposition to receiving foreign rulers, but exhibited it only in tears, which won their affections and secured his affection.

Their former magistrate was still among them as a guardian and example, and was the friend and adviser of his successor. In all civilized societies the acquisition and security of wealth attracts early attention, and is considered the certain proof of wisdom. The new Governor gave early attention to this, and in the most public manner confirmed all the grants that had been made by his predecessor, St. Ange de Bellerive, and, as if to add satisfaction to security, appointed Martin Duvalde, a Frenchman, as surveyor to mark and define their boundaries. He also appointed the late commander of the fort, Capt. Louis St. Ange de Bellerive, a captain in the service of his Catholic Majesty, which still more reconciled them to the change and quieted all their fears for the future, and enabled them to enjoy the fruition of their most sanguine hopes.

The subjects of England, on the east side of the Mississippi river, were soon informed of the liberal policy of the Spanish officers, and began to avail themselves of an exchange of their allegiance for a peaceful home in Missouri, while the opposite side of the river was distracted with frequent murders, raids, battles and desolation.

The wife of Gov. Piernas was a French lady, daughter of Mr. Portneuf, and her relationship and fascinating manners added much to her husband's popularity and enchantment to St. Louis society, which has not as yet entirely faded away. The manners of her husband were formed after the fashion of his own country, having more hauteur than, and less of the familiarity of, the French. This circumstance was near costing him his life, and is the only instance of offense being taken at his conduct in Missouri during the five years he administered the government.

A chief of a tribe of the Osage Indians, being on a visit to the Governor of St. Louis, observed he declined the rude familiarity he had been indulged in by the French, and resolved on assassinating him for the offense. Having collected some chosen followers and decked himself in the fantastic and wild attire of a savage warrior, he returned to St. Louis to put his resolution into execution on the first opportunity. It so happened that a Shawnee chief had then come to St. Louis, with a much larger number of followers, on a treaty for some lands in the rear of Ste. Genevieve, to which they had been invited by Piernas, that he might interpose a barrier between the wild Indians of the West and the settlers of Ste. Genevieve. The Osage, getting into a debauch on the first night of his arrival, boldly declared his intention—that he had come all the distance from his country expressly for that purpose, and only waited for an opportunity to execute his design.

The Shawnee chief, animated by feudal enmity, and exasperated by such nefarious declarations, and willing also to demonstrate his friendship and attachment to Gov. Piernas, drew the Osage into a quarrel and stabbed him to the heart.

He was buried on the high mound which gave name to Mound street, and was then called Grand Terre, and in latter days Big Mound, but which is now entirely removed, and the remains of the Osage chief, as well as other remains, from which they could not be distinguished, scattered.

Many small, rude and trifling ornaments, made of sea and other shells, bone, clay, and two of copper, were also found, but nothing that would enrich a cabinet or add anything to science. The Missouri Historical Society of St. Louis have preserved photographs of it, and observed its removal, to ascertain whether it was the work of nature or art, and have ascertained, beyond a doubt, that it was the work of nature only. The Osages appear never to have noticed the death of the chief. If they did, his death was avenged in secret, as no hostile demonstration was made then or since on their part. The Shawnees and Delawares were assigned lands at that time near Ste. Genevieve, and built villages on them and cultivated them, while the Spanish laws remained in force in the territory.

When Gov. Piernas had administered the government five years with great moderation and satisfaction to the people, he left, amid their tears and benedictions, for New Orleans.

He was succeeded, in 1775, by Don Francisco Cruzat, a most mild and agreeable gentleman, who conducted his administration so quietly in the healthful channels of his predecessor that he was considered a man of very ordinary capacity then, but whom the good and wise will always desire to praise and imitate, as he made all about him happy, contented and prosperous.

It was during this administration that a ferry was established, by John Baptiste Gamasche, across the Merrimac. His family was as remarkable and as much beloved as himself, and has been one of those who have early assisted to form the social, moral and hospitable character of the people. Trade in British goods was so much restricted at that time by the Spanish laws that the people of St. Louis dealt largely in contraband goods, and added much to their commercial profits by smuggling their goods through Cahokia and Kaskaskia. He occupied the same house, on the northeast corner of Main and Walnut streets, which Piernas had done before him; it was one of the first built in St. Louis, and was the seat of hospitality and the high school of fashion during both their administrations.

Three men had now administered the Government in the twelve preceding years to the satisfaction of the governed, and had been sustained by the unfaltering aid and advice of Pierre Laclede Liguest, the founder of the town.

All the inhabitants were contented, prosperous and happy, when, in the summer of 1778, Don Fernando de Leyba, a drunken, avaricious and feeble-minded man, without a single

redeeming qualification, arrived and succeeded Gov. Francisco
Cruzat as Governor.

Great Britain and her colonies were at war. The French and
Spaniards were regarded as allies of the colonies, and liable to
be suddenly attacked at any point. This was the condition of
St. Louis, as developed by the news, on the arrival of Leyba.

To this sad condition of affairs was soon added the report of
the death of Pierre Laclede Liguest, while on a visit to New
Orleans, about midway of his journey.

As his life forms a very interesting part of the history of
St. Louis, no more appropriate place can be selected than this
to describe him as he has generally been represented by his
contemporaries after his death.

Pierre Laclede Liguest was born in Bion, France, near the
base of the Pyrenees mountains, the line between France and
Spain, in the the year 1724. He was about five feet eleven
inches in height, of very dark complexion, black, piercing and
expressive eyes, a large nose, and expansive forehead. He
died on the 20th of June, 1778, in his batteau, on the Mississippi, of a fever, and was buried on the banks of the Mississippi just below its confluence with the Arkansas river, in the
wild solitude of that region, without a stone or tomb to mark
the spot where this enterprising merchant lies.

His history while in Missouri, however, lives, and must live
as long as the city he founded retains its name.

Being of a brave and adventurous disposition, he had collected many followers in his native country for the declared
purpose of establishing a colony in the French possessions in
America. This he fully accomplished in the most peaceful
manner, and in the choice of his location has left a monument
to his wisdom as durable as the rocks on which he built
his city.

He left a host of friends to lament his loss, speak his praise
and enjoy his labors, but no widow to shed a tear or child to
inherit his property or his name.

His partner, Antoine Maxent, a Spanish officer at New
Orleans, got possession of his property and disposed of it in
the following year, 1779, for a trifling sum, and left no slab to
his memory. The inhabitants of the town, presided over by
an unpopular and feeble magistrate, and surrounded by many

warlike omens, became alarmed at their defenseless condition, and, neglecting the cultivation of their grounds, threw up a trench about the town protected by a stockade and pointed brush, with three gates—one on each of the three sides. This, together with a small two-story stone fort, called La Tour, situated near the present junction of Fourth and Walnut streets, formed their feeble defense, and with four small cannons in the fort, were manned with one small company of Spanish soldiers and the citizens generally.

During the first months of the season so many had been employed about the defense that the crops had been much neglected, and fears of a famine in the spring of 1780 began to disturb them more than the fears of Indians, and they went forth to their common fields and planted largely to supply the deficiency of the preceding year.

Early in the spring of this year the British officer in command of Fort Michilimacknac planned an attack on St. Louis, and with four French Canadians who had been in the employment of the Indian fur traders as conductors, named Ducharme, Quennelle, Calvi and Langdon, collected more than one thousand warriors of the Upper Mississippi tribes of Indians to carry it into execution. The warriors assembled according to appointment, and on the morning of the 26th day of May, 1780, crossed the Mississippi a little above the village, near Gingrass creek, and by a circuitous route came upon the early cultivators of the common fields before one-half the laborers had left the village gates. The surprise was mutual. The Indians at finding so few at labor in the common fields, and those nearly all active young men who could run as fast as themselves into town; the villagers at finding themselves attacked at that hour of the day from the rear of the fields. The savages commenced the attack by horrid yells that were heard over the whole village and brought all the men to its defense. The Indians killed forty of the inhabitants and pursued the fugitives to within reach of the cannon from the tower, which had been kept ready, and were discharged on them, and which, by its noise and shot suddenly plowing up the earth near them, frightened them into a retreat to their canoes, when they left the vicinity, taking twelve or fifteen prisoners, most of whom afterward returned.

This massacre was a sad calamity to the village and filled many houses with mourning. Yet there is consolation in looking back on the events of the preceding day and considering how much worse it would have been had the attack been made on the day before in the afternoon.

The day before was the feast of Corpus Christi, a day consecrated by the Catholics with all the religious observances of the Church. In the morning the little church, decorated for the occasion, was crowded by the happy villagers, in their best attire, to hear Father Bernard, the officiating priest. In the afternoon they went in crowds to gather wild strawberries, which were very abundant on the prairie just beyond the common fields. Had the Indians then attacked the village there could have been no doubt of its unhappy fate. The pleasures and amusements of the day, however, caused many to rise later than usual on that next unhappy day, and thus saved their village and their lives. The occurrence gave name to the year, *l'annee du coup*, the year of the blow. Had the Indians been led by one resolute and efficient chief, there can be no doubt their enterprise would have been crowned with complete success. But having been collected by four illiterate and cowardly foreigners, who failed to join them in the attack, the first sign of opposition threw them into a panic, and, like a flock of frightened deer, they fled to their canoes, crossed the Mississippi, and hastened to their remote and scattered homes.

The total failure of the enterprise and the wide-spread report of the frightened savages prevented any further demonstrations by red men against *the high fenced house of thunder*, or the people who lived within hearing of it. This gave the villagers an opportunity of discussing the conduct of their Governor, both before and at the time of the slaughter.

That he was a sot was never questioned; that he had sold the powder of the garrison to some traders before the attack, was proved; and that he used but little precaution to prevent surprise, was apparent from his constantly repelling any idea of a possibility of a surprise. Suggestions were made that he had agreed with the English, for a stipulated sum, to let the savages surprise the town, but it was not necessary to furnish this proof to consign his character to ignominious oblivion and his name, as a Governor, to lasting contempt. Lady Marie de la Conception y Zezar, his wife, had died the autumn before, and was buried in the cemetery of the church, and Don Fernando de Leyba died on the 28th day of June, 1780, and was buried by her side. After his death the duties of Lieutenant-Governor were performed by Lieut. Silvio Francisco Cartabona until the arrival of Don Francisco Cruzat.

On entering upon the administration of the duties of Governor of Upper Louisiana the second time, after an absence of two years, he commenced the regular fortifications of the town, which were a strong stockade of posts, a bastion, and stone forts at proper intervals, which effectually protected the lives and property of the inhabitants of St. Louis from any attacks from savages afterward. It should be borne in mind that Missouri Indians have not destroyed a single hamlet in Missouri or fought a battle on her soil with Europeans. Upper Mississippi Indians, instigated by the British, committed the great massacre of the 20th of May, 1780, without any other cause or provocation.

During the building of the fortifications, and until the peace of 1783, a considerable garrison was maintained, and provisions were dearer in St. Louis than in the towns on the Wabash, whose inhabitants occasionally came to St. Louis to trade, and noticing the high price of bread in particular, which they inferred arose from its scarcity, and to tease the St. Louisians, nick-named their town *Pain Court*, literally, in French, short of bread, which has perpetuated the memory of that fact to this day.

The popularity of the mild and amiable Cruzat, and his liberal policy in former years, attracted many new settlers to Missouri from the French villages of Cahokia and Kaskaskia, and the town was growing apace, when a slow, but most astonishing and irresistible fright fell upon the inhabitants of St. Louis, even greater than the late threatenings of famine and savages. In the early part of the summer of 1785 the Mississippi had risen to it usual hight, but still continued to rise; the whole American Bottom was covered with a sea of swift running water, which bore on its bosom thousands of whole trees, with their roots and branches exposed, accompanied by everything that swollen rivers can bear away, all rushing toward the ocean with a swiftness and majesty that astonished every beholder. The villages of Cahokia and Kaskaskia were surrounded by the rushing waters, sweeping away grain, stock and all the labors of the husbandmen. Still the waters continued to rise and threatened to inundate the town itself and sweep it from existence. Nearly all of the town was then situated on Main street, and when the water had risen above the banks and began to invade their dwellings their terror and apprehensions were very distressing, as there were ancient signs of even higher waters still visible. Just as the inhabitants were about to commence moving their property to the higher bank, where Fourth street now is, the river began to subside and relieve their fears, after having taught them that it is possible for the river to rise much higher than they saw it and yet leave them a place of safety.

This year was denominated by the French l'annee des grands eaux (the year of great waters). Many persons who had been compelled by the high water to leave the American Bottom, on the subsidence of the waters made St. Louis their abode, and assisted in giving activity to its growth and character to its inhabitants, as they were mostly peaceful Canadian Creoles. Such was the character of the people of St. Louis that, during the French and Spanish domination, but one murder was committed, and that was perpetrated by a Spanish soldier on one of his comrades, whom he had stabbed to the heart in a sudden quarrel, for which he was immediately ironed and sent to New Orleans for trial. Though the commerce of St. Louis was never disturbed by the Indians, yet it was much damaged after the close of the American Revolutionary war by piratical bands of lawless white men, runaway negroes, mulattoes and half-breed Indians.

These marauders became the terror of Mississippi boatmen and merchants navigating the river for several years. They generally located themselves in the vicinity of the Grand Tower, a rock fifty feet in hight, located about midway between the mouths of the Missouri and Ohio rivers, where the Mississippi is confined by solid rocks to one swift channel near its base, at which point those navigating barges up stream were generally in the habit of going along the shore in advance of their barges and drawing them with ropes along near the shore. Near this pass the pirates would lurk and suddenly attack the navigators when off their guard, seize the merchandize and leave no one to tell the tale.

These acts gave rise to many sad and romantic tales, related about the hearths and camp fires of the early settlers of Missouri.

One of the most interesting forms a part of the history of Missouri and St. Louis, and was written by Hon. Wilson Primm, present Judge of the St. Louis Criminal Court, more than thirty years ago, while he was a law student, and while yet many persons still live in St. Louis who knew the parties and could verify most of the facts. It was read by himself before the members of the St. Louis Lyceum, in 1838, and in his own words, connected with his name, goes down to posterity as the real history of the past:

"A band of pirates were located at Cottonwood creek, commanded by two men named Culbert and Mogilbray. In the spring of 1787 a barge belonging to Mr. Beausolid had started from New Orleans richly laden with merchandise for St. Louis. As she approached Cottonwood creek a breeze sprang up and bore it swiftly by. This the robbers perceived, and immediately dispatched a company of men up the river for the purpose of heading it. The maneuver was effected in the course of two days at an island, which has since been called Beausolid Island. The barge had just pushed ashore; the robbers boarded and ordered the crew to return down. The men were disarmed; guards were stationed in every part of the vessel, and she was soon under way. Mr. Beausolid gave himself up to despair. He had all he possessed in the purchase of the barge and its cargo, and now that he was to be deprived of them all he was in agony.

"The vessel would have shared the fate of many others that had preceded it but for the heroic daring of a negro who was one of the crew. Casotte, the negro, was a man rather under the ordinary hight, very slender in person, but of extraordinary strength and activity. The color of his skin and curl of his hair alone told that he was a negro, for the peculiar characteristics of his race had given place in him to what might be termed beauty. His forehead was finely moulded, his eyes small and sparkling as those of a serpent, his nose aquiline, his lips of proper thickness; in fact the whole appearance of the man, joined to his known character for shrewdness and courage, seemed to indicate that under better circumstances he might have shown conspicuously in the history of nations.

"Casotte, as soon as the robbers had taken possession of the barge, began to make every demonstration of uncontrollable joy. He danced, sang, laughed, and soon induced his captors to believe that they had delivered him from irksome slavery, and that his actions were the ebullitions of pleasure. His constant attention to all their smallest wants and wishes won their confidence, and whilst they kept a watchful eye on the other prisoners, they permitted him to roam through the vessel unmolested and unwatched.

"This was the state of things that the negro desired. He seized the first opportunity to speak to Mr. Beausolid, and beg permission to rid him of his dangerous intruders. He laid his plan before his master, who, after a great deal of hesitation, acceded to it. Casotte then spoke to two of the crew, likewise negroes, and engaged them in the conspiracy. Casotte was cook, and it was agreed between him and his fellow-conspirators that the signal for dinner should be the signal for action.

"The hour of dinner at length arrived. The robbers assembled in considerable numbers on the deck and stationed themselves at the bow and stern and along the sides, to prevent any rising of the men. Casotte went among them with the most unconscious look and demeanor imaginable. As soon as he perceived his comrades had taken the stations he had assigned them, he took his position at the bow of the boat, near one of the robbers, a stout, herculean man, armed cap-a-pie. Everything being arranged to his satisfaction, Casotte gave the preconcerted signal, and immediately the robber near him was struggling in the water. With the speed of lightning he went from one robber to another, and in less than three minutes he had thrown fourteen of them overboard. Then seizing an oar he struck on the head those who attempted to save themselves by grappling the running boards, then shot with the muskets that had been dropped on deck those who swam away. In the meantime, the other conspirators were not idle, but did almost as much execution as their leader. The deck was soon cleared, and the robbers that remained below were too few in number to offer any resistance. Having got rid of his troublesome visitors, Mr. Beausolid deemed it prudent to return to New Orleans. This he accordingly did, taking care when he arrived at Cottonwood creek to keep the opposite side of the river.

"He reached New Orleans and gave an account of his capture and liberation to the Governor, who therefore issued an order that the boats bound for St. Louis in the following spring should all go in company, to afford mutual assistance in case of necessity. Spring came, and ten keel boats, each provided with swivels and their respective crews well armed, took their departure from New Orleans, determined, if possible, to destroy most of the robbers. When they neared the Cottonwood creek the foremost boat perceived several men near the mouth among the trees. The anchor was dropped and she waited until the other boats should come up. In a few moments they appeared, and a consultation was held, in which it was determined that a sufficient number of men should remain on board whilst the others should proceed on shore to attack the robbers. The boats were rowed to shore in line, and those appointed for that purpose landed and began to search the island in quest of the robbers in vain. They had disappeared. Three or four flat-boats were found in the bend of the creek, laden with all kinds of valuable merchandise, the fruits of their depredations. A long, low hut was discovered—the dwelling of the robbers—in which were stowed away numerous cases of guns, destined for the fur trade, and ammunition and provisions of all kinds. The greater part of these things were put on board the boats and restored to their respective owners in St. Louis. This proceeding had the effect of dispersing the robbers, for they were never after heard of. The arrival of ten barges together at St. Louis was an unusual spectacle, and the year 1788 has ever since been called *l'anee des dix bateaux* (the year of the ten boats). In this year the authority of Francisco Cruzat ceased. His administrations had both been mild, but not brilliant. He had fortified the town and made its position widely known and permanent. It had thereby become the repository of the valuable merchandise that was to supply the vast regions to the north and west, the bounds of which were not known. He left lasting marks of the interest he felt in the safety and welfare of those he governed, and retired without a stain on his peaceful and quiet character. The town and surrounding villagers included in the St. Louis district then contained eleven hundred and ninety-seven inhabitants, and the district of Ste. Genevieve eight hundred, exclusive of the Shawnee and Delaware Indians, who, on the invitation of Governor Piernas, were then essaying agriculture and had several small villages in that vicinity. Don Manuel Perez succeeded Governor Cruzat as Commandant General of Upper Louisiana, and both he and his family were so much like Governor Cruzat and his family that the difference in their names was about all the change the peaceful people of St. Louis could perceive. They pursued their usual avocations and amusements with the same zest and pleasure as before, and with the same happy and beneficial results.

"The merchants of St. Louis enjoyed two markets, one by New Orleans, the other by Canada, after the peace of 1783, and feared no hostile attack from Indians. Yet, from policy and prudence, the commandant, to carry out the already begun scheme of Gov. Piernas to interpose the Shawnee and Delaware Indians between the feeble settlements and the Western Indians, who, although they never made war or a direct attack upon a large scale, lurked about the settlement and frequently killed an indiscreet inhabitant found wandering too far from town. He employed a Mr. Lorimer in this business and effected his object, and Mr. Lorimer received a grant of thirty thousand acres of land as his reward.

"The Indians also received large tracts and settled on them, near Cape Girardeau, and partially fulfilled their engagements as to affording protection from other Indians, but occasionally committed the same outrages themselves they had engaged to prevent. Thus one of the inhabitants of St. Louis—one of the present well known family of Duchouquette—was set upon while alone near Chouteau's pond, by a small party of the Delawares, then called by the French *Les Loups* (wolves), murdered and scalped. His brother, Francis Duchouquette, was at some distance and saw the Indians kill him, and immediately brought the news to town. Officer Tayon, with a company of men, started in immediate pursuit, and, taking a circuitous route, came unexpectedly upon the party, when Duchouquette, singling out the Indian who had killed his brother, and whose scalp hung at his belt, shot him in the thigh, which felled him to the ground. He was soon despatched by a soldier, and four more of the party killed in the pursuit. This act of the Delawares, at the threshold of the Governor's headquarters, ruined the character of the Delawares, and the Shawnees suffered a loss of confidence. They were no longer desired as neighbors, confided in as friends, or respected as men, but feared, distrusted and shunned, until they abandoned their village and lands and returned to the forests and the chase."

CHAPTER III.

The Happy Days of St. Louis and Missouri—The Transfer of the Country from Spain to France, and from France to the United States.

The administration of Manuel Perez, as Commandant General of the post of St. Louis, extended from 1788 to 1793, and was so mild and satisfactory that the people appear, at this day, to have obtained from him all they desired, and to have rewarded him by the most perfect conformity to his wishes, so that we are now unable to determine which party was best pleased, the governor or the governed. He was very liberal, and, so far as we can discover, granted them all the lands they desired, and encouraged foreigners to participate in his bounties like his own people.

When Zenon Trudeau, his successor, arrived, he resigned his authority to him with as much apparent pleasure as he had performed any other duty, and retired with the love and respect of all his people.

The people had become so much accustomed to kind rulers that they received their new magistrate with apparent pleasure, and seem never to have had the least occasion to regret the change. Indeed, he walked so uniformly in the steps of his predecessor that no change was perceptible in the administration of those two amiable officers.

The prosperity and happiness of the people are the best records of both their administrations. When the Commandant

General, Trudeau, entered on the performance of the duties of his office he seemed to be performing the labors his predecessor had laid ont for him, only he enlarged the scale.

The fear of the Indians daily decreased, and white men pushed their enterprises still further into the wilderness and enlarged their farms and flocks. Extraordinary inducements were offered to settlers on the Spanish domain. Large grants of land were made to citizens of the United States and intercourse encouraged.

There were no mails or taverns, but every house was a welcome home to the new comers, for some one was to hear from distant friends and the outside world. Therefore the stranger was an acquisition, not a burden, in every house, and his society sought for and appreciated. Business and trades of all kinds were extended and encouraged.

Huts gave place to houses, moccasins to shoes, and the chase to agriculture. Large and more frequent surveys were made, and new fields and new villages occupied the former haunts of the buffalo and elk.

His family was as much beloved and respected as himself, and both mingled with the people as though all of the same family without exhibiting any external marks of distinction, while their people seemed about to overwhelm them with attention and kindness. This popular officer also retired with the universal regret of all his people, from an office which they would have wished to have him fill during life, and died at New Orleans a few years later. It is seldom that an important office is filled so many times in succession with a popular incumbent. St. Louis, however, had been singularly fortunate in its first magistrate during the three last administrations; although nothing transcendantly brilliant had been accomplished, still the people appear to have enjoyed all they desired.

The beloved Zenon Trudeau was succeeded in 1708 by Charles Dehault Delassus de Delusiere, a native of France, who had been long in the Spanish service, and was promoted to the office of Lieutenant Governor of Upper Louisiana, from being Commandant of the Post of New Madrid, in reward of his long and faithful services in the army.

The first act of his administration was to show the prosperous condition his predecessor had left the country in, by at once taking the census, which showed the population to amount to six thousand and twenty-eight, of which one thousand and eighty were colored.

This exposition of the faithful administration of his predecessor confirmed him in the esteem of the people, which he retained for the quarter of a century that followed in which he was a most conspicuous actor.

The wars of Europe, the uncertain tenure of title to the territory and office, the mixed laws of the two countries, and the numberless interests requiring attention, kept the mind of the Governor brilliant and active. He was a gentleman of the most agreeable and fascinating manners, and bore one of the kindest and lightest hearts that ever filled a Frenchman's bosom. Moreover, he was unmarried, and had power to make unlimited grants of land in all the territory of Upper Louisiana.

Tradition says, St. Louis belles and land lovers had the same propensities then, and used the same arts and arguments as at this day to win attentions and rich concessions, and the result was natural. The bachelor Governor obtained the hand of the prettiest lady, and land-seekers the choicest tracts in the territory. The price of occupying those grants was frequently the hazard of their lives for years, although there was no open war. The wilderness was all traveled over by explorers for mines and choice locations, and the office of the Governor was filled and surrounded by speculators and carpet-baggers at that early day as the offices at Washington are at this, and for the same selfish purposes. The administration of Gov. Delassus closed with the Spanish domination in Louisiana, and had been conducted with such wisdom, kindness and success, that he laid down his authority on the transfer of the country to the United States with apparent pleasure, and with his young family took his position as an American citizen among the people, and continued his residence in St. Louis for the next twenty years. The three administrations immediately preceding his had been so very mild, peaceful and popular that it seemed to require a quarter of a century to excel all of them.

He, however, accomplished it in five years of his administration, and then enjoyed twenty years of sweet repose among those whom he had benefited all in his power. How few among men ever enjoy such a reward! It may afford pleasure to some to learn that his son has returned from France and is making Missouri his home, and showing by his benevolence the traits of his ancestry.

The United States authority in Missouri dates from the 10th day of March, 1804. There were then in the Territory ten thousand three hundred and forty inhabitants, of which one thousand three hundred and twenty were colored.

The village of St. Louis contained one hundred and eighty houses, built of hewn logs and stone, the latter being generally the residences of the most wealthy, and surrounded by a wall of the same material, enclosing the whole block, which continued in use many years protecting the fine fruit trees which shaded the mansion. Soon after the change of government the mode of building with wood changed, and frame houses became fashionable and common, and logs went out of use as building materials. There were but one bakery, two small taverns, three blacksmiths, two mills and one doctor in the town. Wood was the only fuel used. No brick had then been made, or a street paved or graded. The village, however, was well supplied with merchants, but they held their goods at enormous prices. Coffee and sugar each at two dollars per pound, and everything else in proportion. Their places of business were very much scattered, and commonly in the family mansion of each, in which one might find the greatest variety of goods, from a fish-hook to a lexicon.

This was the condition of St. Louis on the 10th of March, 1804, when Major Amos Stoddard assumed the duties of Governor of Upper Louisiana, with all the authority of a Spanish commandant, and occupied the government house on the northeast corner of Main and Walnut streets. He was an officer of great merit and ability, and fulfilled his duties satisfactorily for the short time he held the office. Sixteen days after he assumed the duties of the office, Congress, on the 26th day of March, 1804, divided the Louisiana province into two parts by the thirty-third parallel of latitude, and placed the northern district under the domination of Indiana, then including Illinois. This act of Congress was at once promulgated, and filled the people with astonishment and alarm, as they had not got through with reading the circular address of their new Governor before this office was abolished, and their government turned over to a new lot of strangers residing beyond the Wabash river. They were, however, consoled by the presence of both their late Governors and their Secretaries, with their families, one of which was the late Hon. M. Philip Leduc, who so often filled responsible offices in after years, both under the Territorial and State governments.

So cheering is the reminiscences of such people and their beneficent acts that it is difficult to pass on in the history without a more full description of them. It was the presence of such people that made life tolerable, and, indeed, happy under such circumstances, and gave character, progress and refinement to society in those days.

Capt. Merriwether Lewis and Lieut. William Clarke had an exploring expedition then preparing at the mouth of Wood river, in Illinois, above St. Louis, to make their celebrated journey by the Missouri and Columbia rivers to the Pacific Ocean.

The party left their encampment on the 14th of May, 1804, and were joined at St. Charles, on the 21st, by Capt. Lewis, the commander from St. Louis, to which place he returned after an absence of two years, four months and two days. This expedition somewhat diverted the attention of the people from their political affairs until the Presidential election in the States (in which they could take no part) began to threaten further changes. The stability and peaceful disposition of the people, in the presence of so many of their former officers, caused society to move forward, as if by its own momentum, in its old channels. In August, after the departure of Lewis and Clarke's expedition, Lieut. Zebulon Pike left his encampment, near St. Louis, to explore the Mississippi river to its source. The fitting out of these two expeditions, the opening of the Mississippi to free navigation, the influx of strangers and the establishment of a postoffice, created so much excitement that no complaints were made against the Government until the arrival of Gov. Wm. H. Harrison, of Indiana, whose duty it was to preside over this extensive district, which lately was under four different officers, acting as commandants—one at

New Madrid, Don Juan Lavallie; one at Ste. Genevieve, Don Francis Valle; one at Cape Girardeau, Don Louis Lorimer, and the Commandant General at St. Louis. Gov. Harrison met with the most kind reception, on his arrival, from all the inhabitants, and received every assurance of their most cordial support and obedience.

Having learned the wants of the people, he returned, and, with the Judge of the territory of Indiana, on 1st of October, 1804, passed such acts as were deemed necessary for the new district. His last official act for the district appears to have been performed on the 24th of April, 1805. Congress, however, on the 3d of March, 1805, had changed the name of the District of Louisiana to the Territory of Louisiana, and at the passage of the act, Gen. James Wilkinson was appointed Governor of the territory, and soon entered on the discharge of the duties of the office.

The purchase of Louisiana from France by the United States, for fifteen millions of dollars, had now become known through Europe and America, and was received as a great and important movement, and naturally attracted the eyes of the enterprising to the wide field spread before them.

The temperate climate of Upper Louisiana invited all to examine and consider its magnitude, productions and attractions. St. Louis being the most accessible point from which to explore its vast regions, was visited by great numbers of travelers, traders and adventurers of every description, as the reputation of the heterogeneous population of the town promised fellowship to all classes, castes and colors.

Even the celebrated Aaron Burr thought it worthy of a visit from him, and the tender of his patronage to its highest officer.

All these united to increase the notoriety of St. Louis and accelerate its growth. The indiscretion of Burr, however, led him to so far unmask his designs that Gov. Wilkinson was ordered to watch his traitorous movements in person, which withdrew him from his duties as Governor of the Territory. In the meantime the expedition of Lewis and Clarke had returned from the Pacific Ocean and filled the country with their fame. To fill the office now vacant by the withdrawal of Gen. Wilkinson, Capt. Merriwether Lewis was appointed Governor of the Territory by the President, and hailed with universal approbation. In all these changes the public peace, or course of business and amusements, had not been checked or disturbed; on the contrary, the kindest and most hospitable feeling everywhere manifested itself. New comers were regarded as acquisitions, and aided in locating themselves in comfortable quarters and finding employment. If they had families they were visited, and taken by the hand as friends who merited attention, encouragement and patronage from every citizen. While these mighty changes were silently going on among men to improve and govern themselves, the Mississippi was as silently making changes to accommodate itself, which has resulted in most wonderfully increasing the labor of establishing a government for it beyond the calculations of the most scientific at the commencement of this century.

At that time the Mississippi was narrow and swift in front of the village, and washed the limestone bluff from the northeast of the Spanish fortress to Market street, from thence to the mouth of Mill creek, near the southeast Spanish stone fort—(the sight of the gasworks). It passed in a straight channel about seventy-five feet deep, the shores being so near each other that the calls of people from the opposite shore could be distinctly heard. There had then been no such lands as Bloody Island, Duncan's Island, or Arsenal Island. They are deposits made by the river in the present century.

A heavily timbered tract of land, about half a mile wide, covered the site of Bloody Island and East St. Louis, which was gradually washed away, and the river widened thereby, causing a corresponding decrease in the velocity of the stream, and the formation of bars and islands at other places. The place of crossing the Mississippi from Cahokia was for many years from that place to the present Arsenal tract, where there was and still is a good landing on low rocky ledges.

In 1792 and 1793 the small stream L'Abbe, or Cahokia creek, being frozen, Judge Pigott, of St. Clair county, Illinois, essayed to build a bridge across the stream opposite St. Louis. The stream was then only one hundred and fifty feet wide, and Judge Pigott an enterprising and energetic man, yet so herculean was that labor that with his small means he spent three winters at the bridge, and finished it in 1795, after Gen. Wayne had subdued the confederate Indians at Anglaize, or Miami.

Tradition says he had chopped down most of the trees to build it with his own hands, while his rifle leaned against another tree, prepared to be used on the Indian foes who, during the first two winters, swarmed on the prairies of Illinois, Indiana and Ohio. Having built two log cabins, and hollowed and burned out some Indian canoes or pirogues, and put a platform on a pair of them for carrying teams during the next two years, he was ready, in 1797, to apply to that good Governor, Zenon Trudeau, for a license for establishing the *first*, and what is *now* the Wiggins, ferry.

His success, on application, was such as comported with the character of the two gentlemen. The Governor not only granted his petition, but went further, making him a citizen and granting him permission to put his ferry-house on the *place d'armes*, near the east end of Market street, where he continued his ferry until his death, in 1799.

The name of Captain James Pigott deserves a high place among the early benefactors of St. Louis for this act, as it opened a direct communication between the city and the opposite shore, whereas, before the establishment of his ferry, the only means of crossing was in bateaux from near Cahokia to the present U. S. Arsenal grounds. An island was then located near the Illinois shore, extending from opposite where the East St. Louis Elevator now stands to opposite the Arsenal grounds, having a swift, narrow chute on the east side.

The Mississippi at that period had no other obstruction from Bissell's Point to Carondelet. In 1800 a small sandbar made its appearance near the Illinois shore just below the point, and deflected a portion of the river more directly on the Illinois shore, which was then covered with a dense forest of the largest trees usually found in the American Bottom from the river to the L'Abbe or Cahokia creek, distant half a mile eastwardly. This tongue of land was also thickly overgrown with grape and wild pea vines, and afforded shelter for the Indians who came to trade at St. Louis, and forage for their horses, and at a later period for cattle.

The large trees growing near the water began to be undermined, and falling into the river floated away, expanding the channel on the east of the bar, affording a constantly increasing current, which at the end of the first quarter of this century had washed away so much of the alluvial soil of Illinois that half of the Mississippi passed on the east of the bar or Bloody Island, as it had now come to be called on account of several duels having been fought on it.

In the meantime its location had become greatly changed and its size increased. The upper end had greatly washed away and the middle expanded; large deposits of sand had been made at the lower end by each flood, until, at the end of the half century, it divided the Mississippi in two nearly equal parts, and presented its western shore on the same place where the Illinois shore was in 1800. It formed a striking feature in front of a great city, and caused the old natives to review the wonderful changes they had witnessed. The old, narrow channel of the Mississippi, that was seventy-five feet deep in 1800, was occupied by Duncan's Island, and steamboats grounded in front of the old village site of that date.

The island that once covered the Illinois shore opposite the lower part of the city had long since been washed away, and Arsenal Island, and other obstructions to navigation near the city, had presented themselves, which have since taxed the wisdom of the learned to avoid herculean labor or the loss of the river.

We return to our direct history of the city, having by our digression presented, as we think, a necessary description of the features of the river.

The administration of James Wilkinson, as Governor of the Territory of Louisiana, commenced at St. Louis, May 6, 1806. He had associated with him, in the performance of his legislative duties, Hon. John B. C. Lucas and Return J. Meigs, Jr.; Judge Joseph Browne, Secretary.

They passed seven public acts, and each signed the acts, with his name to each particular act. The last act was dated July 9th, 1806.

Gov. James Wilkinson was then ordered by President Jefferson to leave the territory and watch the movements of the ex-Vice-President, Aaron Burr. The duties of the Governor then devolved on the Secretary of the Territory, Joseph Browne.

In the meantime Hon. Otho Shrader had taken the place of Judge Meigs, and their first act was passed October 28th, 1806, and signed Joseph Browne, John B. C. Lucas, Otho Shrader.

This appears to have been the last official act of Secretary Browne, and the only one where he acted ex officio as Governor. Hon. Frederick Bates was appointed Secretary of the territory, and on the 7th of May, 1807, signed his first act as acting Governor in legislation, assisted by Judges Lucas and Shrader. These gentlemen passed several acts during the year, and in one of them the name of Judge John Coburn appears among them as officiating in legislation.

On the 30th of April, 1806, Lieut. Zebulon M. Pike returned to St. Louis from exploring the Mississippi to its source. He was soon after ordered, by Gov. Wilkinson, to prepare for escorting and returning to their former friends and relatives fifty-one Osage and Pawnee Indians, who had been redeemed from captivity among the Pottawatomies, by the United States. This order, dated June 21st, 1806, was followed by another dated July 12th, 1806, and, together, formed the instructions which resulted in his being apprehended with his party in the Spanish territory, and conducted to Mexico, from whence he returned to Natchitoches, on July 1st, 1807.

These acts of kindness and humanity explain why those two powerful nations were always friendly with Missourians.

As an evidence that it was not by largesses they dwelt in peace with white men, we have Gov. Wilkinson's letter to Lieut. Pike, in which he says:

"To disburse your necessary expenses and to aid your negotiations, you are herewith furnished *six hundred* dollars worth of goods, for the appropriation of which you are to render a *strict* account, vouched by documents to be attested by one of your party."

Before the result of Gov. Wilkinson's investigations had developed the design of Aaron Burr, the expedition under Lewis and Clarke had returned from exploring the Missouri and Columbia rivers, and they had taken up their residence in St. Louis.

President Jefferson, well knowing the qualifications of Capt. Lewis to fill the office of Governor of a territory of such vast extent, peopled, as most of it was, by Indians who knew his character and appreciated it, appointed him to that office early in 1807, which gave universal satisfaction to the people, as he was a very popular and agreeable gentleman. The progress of improvement in those early days was not rapid. The age of invention had not arrived with the advent of Americans.

A postoffice was established in 1804, with a mail once in each week to Cahokia, and the communication with Illinois was considered easy then.

The Pigott Ferry was kept in operation and well patronized, and one was also in limited operation below the village. The exports from the territory, however, consisted of lead, furs and peltries only.

The increase in population was slow, being 925 in 1799, and 11 years after only 1,400—in 1810.

The embargo of 1807, and the non-intercourse with England of 1809, had a withering influence on the prosperity of St. Louis, as on other commercial towns. Yet its attractions were not entirely hidden from the eyes of far-seeing men. When the embargo had prostrated almost every enterprise throughout the country, Mr. Joseph Charles, in July, 1808, commenced the publication of a weekly newspaper, which is the present *Missouri Republican*, and has not missed an issue at the appointed time since, and is its own historian now.

The gloom that hung over commercial affairs then seemed to give very great uneasiness to all engaged in the fur trade at that period, and none appeared more affected by it than Gov. Lewis. Deep sympathy with his suffering people seemed to have seized upon him. His friends used all the means that friendship could suggest to rouse him from mental depression, for which they saw no other cause.

At length, early in the autumn of 1809, they persuaded him to visit Louisville, and while on his journey thither he deliberately destroyed his life with his own pistol. He was pitied and mourned as his worth deserved. His explorations had furnished a lasting monument to his memory, and materials for many elegies as tributes to his virtues and exploits. He left no family to be afflicted by his unnatural end, but many sincere, sympathizing friends.

The pacific disposition of the Indians and attractions of the as yet unoccupied lands of Missouri had caused its whole surface to be explored for mines and minerals so thoroughly that the few who were disposed to labor found no difficulty in obtaining employment in business suited to their taste and capacity.

There was probably never a happier or more contented people than the Missourians until some one became rich enough to live without labor. The law-abiding disposition of the early settlers is prominently exhibited by the fact that there was not a single conviction for murder during the first half century of its settlement, and half the houses of the inhabitants had no locks in them or on them. The first public execution for murder in Missouri was that of a young man for deliberately shooting his step-father, which was on the 16th of September, 1808, at St. Louis. Until the titles to grants of lands made by Spanish officers had been confirmed by the United States' Commissioners very few attempts had been made to develop the mineral wealth of the territory, except in the lead regions, where small capital and skill were requisite. When most of the grants had been confirmed, and surveys made of public lands, and offices opened for their sale, the whole face of the country exhibited a visible change. Large square fields began to occupy the prairies and dwellings to dot the fringes of timber. The mines were wrought more skillfully and with machinery. The salt springs in Howard county, bearing the name of "Boonslick," from the great Kentucky woodsman, Daniel Boone, require a special notice in connection with Missouri's early history. For many years after the formation of the territorial government over Missouri the Boonslick country was the great centre of attraction to all emigrants seeking new homes on the west of the Mississippi. The fame of the salt works of Major James Morrison, conducted with such wonderful energy, skill, and success, had made it a point from which many travelers commenced their explorations and inquiries, and few places ever presented more wide-spread and fascinating prospects than this, or ever more bountifully repaid the advances made for its improvement.

One of the first offices opened by the United States for the sale of lands on the west side of the Mississippi was in the vicinity of Boonslick, in 1818, and none was ever more overwhelmingly thronged with purchasers of the lands they were already cultivating. Some of these had located themselves on the public domain as soon as it had been purchased by the

United States, and, foregoing personal safety and the comforts of refined society, had plunged into the wilderness, and made their own home with their own hands. They had obeyed the territorial laws as required, and watched and protected its interests as their own.

On the death of Gov. Merriwether Lewis, President James Madison appointed Benjamin Howard Governor of the Territory of Louisiana, whose first legislative act was signed October 25th, 1810, and his last October 31st, 1810. It has been a subject of universal remark that the people of Missouri were more satisfactorily governed without representation than they ever have since they elected their own Legislators. More than fifty years had now elapsed since the first settlement of Missouri, and yet the people had approved of all the acts of all their rulers except Leyba.

The administration of Governor Howard was short, but very satisfactory to the people.

He resigned his office as Governor of the Territory to accept the office of Brigadier-General of Rangers in the war of 1812, and, having served with great credit to himself during three campaigns, died at St. Louis September 18, 1814.

On his resignation, Capt. William Clarke, the companion of Capt. Lewis on the celebrated exploring expedition of the Missouri and Columbia rivers, was appointed Governor of the Territory. Missouri had been raised to the second grade of territorial government, and elected its own House of Representatives, and the President appointed the Council, with the approval of the Senate.

The first legislative act under Gov. Clarke's administration was approved on the 31st of December, 1813. George Bullet was then Speaker of the House and S. Hammond was President of the Council. Gov. Clarke's administration continued until Missouri was admitted as a member of the Federal Union.

The resignation of the office by Gov. Howard arose from his desire to render more efficient military service to his country in the capacity of a military chief than he could do as Governor in the struggle that his far-seeing eye noticed gathering about the Territory and disturbing and destroying its prosperity. He was not alone in the movements of the day for the general safety of the people. At that time Illinois had been detached from Indiana by an act of Congress of February 3, 1809, and the Governors of the three Territories of Indiana, Illinois and Missouri were all watching the movements and machinations of Tecumseh and his brother, Elshnatann, the prophet, with great solicitude, and making every preparation in their power, in unison with each other, to protect and defend their people and their property.

CHAPTER IV.

Raid on Loutre Island by the Indians, and Death of several Prominent Citizens—The Battle of Tippecanoe, and the First Steamboat on the Western Rivers, in 1811—The Great Earthquake and Destruction of New Madrid.

The purchase of Louisiana from France by the United States had not only changed the officers of the Government, but substituted another code of laws. This entirely changed the mode of obtaining titles to lands, or rather stopped their acquisition from Government for many years after.

Under the French and Spanish dominations lands were always conveyed by grants and never by sales, and these grants were made with certain official formalities which required months to accomplish them.

At the time of the purchase many of the grants lacked some of the official formalities which made them valid. Congress, in 1806, had this under consideration, and appointed three commissioners to examine and confirm them. Hon. John B. C. Lucas, Clement B. Penrose and James L. Donaldson were at first appointed; but, in 1807, Frederick Bates was appointed in the place of James L. Donaldson. Their duties were found to be laborious, unpleasant and tedious, as most of the formalities were imperfect, the grants doubtful and conflicting, and the interests involved great. It resulted, after long delay, in Congress aiding the claimants in perfecting all the grants not deemed fraudulent in the inception.

These imperfect claims had greatly retarded the improvement of some of the most valuable lands in the State, and deprived owners of the enjoyment of their grants beyond the period of their lives.

The most friendly relations existed between the settlers and Indians living south of the Missouri river, while danger was apprehended from those residing north of it, as they were supplied with goods by British traders, and were much under their influence. Moreover, their fears had been excited by a report made by Mr. Nicholas Jarrot, of Cahokia, under oath, of what he had noticed on 28th June, 1809, at Prairie du Chien. Soon after a demonstration was made on Fort Madison, Iowa, by the Fox Indians, which showed more clearly the hostile designs of the Northern Indians. In the month of August, 1809, a party of Iowas killed several Osages near Liberty, on the north of the Missouri.

The latter attempted to retaliate, and in their reconnoitering excursions found the Iowas well supplied with new British arms and plenty of ammunition, of which the frontier settlers were soon made aware by their frequent losses of cattle and horses.

At length, in July, 1810, a party of Indians, supposed to be Pottawatomies, came to the settlement of Loutre Island, near the mouth of Gasconade river, and stole several horses. A party of six persons immediately started in pursuit, consisting of Stephen Cooper, Samuel Cole, William T. Cole and Messrs. Brown, Gooch and Patton, who, following the Indians across the grand prairie to a branch of Salt river, then called Bonelick, discovered them (eight in number) retreating and casting away their plunder. Night coming on, the party encamped and slept without a sentinel, and, as should have reasonably been expected, were attacked by the savages and half their number slain. The Indians also lost four of their number killed and wounded, but they kept the property of both parties and the field. This roused the settlers to greater vigilance, and made every person capable of bearing arms a soldier and every house a fortress for the next five years, and nearly suspended all improvements.

The three Territories of Indiana, Illinois and Louisiana were then presided over by three officers of about equal ability. Either was very able to lead in battle or preside over a Senate.

It seldom happens that three such persons as William Henry Harrison, Ninian Edwards and Benjamin Howard are all found in the right place so near each other in such an important crisis. They were, however, always in place, and they acted as one mind and carried all their friends with them. They saw the impending danger and prepared to meet it in the best manner, and succeeded. General Harrison, who was best known to Tecumseh—an ambitious chief and leader among the malcontent Indians on the east of the Mississippi—had convened a council on the 15th of August, 1811, composed of about fifty of the most turbulent and restless chiefs, with the view of quieting their dissatisfaction or settling their claims. The council was abruptly dissolved and hasty preparations made by both parties for war. The three Governors, acting in unison, aided and assisted each other in such a manner that their whole available resources were exerted on the point requiring support in this crisis.

On the 7th of November, 1811, Gen. Harrison defeated the Indians at Tippecanoe, which quieted them for a time, and gave a respite from thefts, raids and murders in all three of the Territories until the declaration of war against Great Britain, June 19, 1812. The watchfulness of the people, however, was not in the least abated, for it was known that the battle had been fought and lost without the presence or approbation of their greatest chief, and that Tecumseh would make another effort, in person, with the scattered warriors, as soon as he could again inspire them with courage and get them united.

The people of Missouri had scarce heard the tale of the battle and rejoiced over the victory when, on the night of the 16th of December, 1811, they were aroused from their slumbers by an earthquake that shook the whole valley of the Mississippi, destroyed the town of New Madrid, and filled every reasonable creature with consternation and horror. A series of shocks followed and vast chasms opened, from whence issued columns of water, sand and coal, then closed, and the earth rocked to and fro while flashes of electricity gleamed through the troubled clouds, rendering the darkness of night more terrific. These shocks continued at intervals several weeks, lessening in violence, but leaving lasting traces of its ruinous effects, such as stagnant lakes and ponds where whole farms and sections had sunk several feet and filled with fetid water, loathsome to all living creatures. The terrified occupants fled from the vicinity of their former homes, while hissings and rumbling sounds like distant thunder accelerated their flight and discouraged their return. A dense, black cloud of vapor hung over the earth and partially hid the sun from view by day and rendered night doubly dark and dreary, while the air resounded with the cries of wild animals on land and birds on wing in search of a more safe and quiet resting place.

The central point of this remarkable convulsion in nature seems to have been near the site of New Madrid, in the southeast corner of the State, and slight shocks and undulations were frequently felt in that vicinity for half a century afterward. Congress, at a subsequent day, partially remunerated the sufferers by this appalling phenomenon in grants of public lands.

These grants or certificates were issued at an early period, and form the titles to some of the most valuable tracts of land in the State. Another remarkable event was coincident with this earthquake, and aids in making 1811 a memorable epoch among the people of the West.

Mr. Roosevelt, of New York, during this year, built the first steamboat that ever floated on the Western rivers, at the city of Pittsburgh, and named it New Orleans, and navigated it safely into the Mississippi, and was lying moored to its shore when the vessel was nearly overwhelmed by the agitation of the waters and earthquake. It, however, arrived safely at its destination, and opened a new era for Missouri and the West. The battle of Tippecanoe, the great earthquake, and the first steamboat all occurred in the year 1811, and will be long remembered in the Western States. An act of Congress was approved June 4th, 1813, which changed the name of the Territory of Louisiana to that of Missouri, and advanced it to the second grade of government after the first Monday of December of that year. Gov. Howard organized the Territory into five counties, as it had been in districts before, and by proclamation on the first of October ordered an election to be held on the second Monday in November, for a delegate to Congress and members of a House of Representatives.

Edward Hempstead was elected delegate to Congress at this

session. The House of Representatives commenced their first session on the 7th day of December, 1812, and after the organization (the oath of office being administered by Hon. John B. C. Lucas, one of the judges), the House of Representatives proceeded to nominate eighteen persons, from whom the President of the United States, with the Senate, selected nine for the council of the Territory.

The acting governor, Frederick Bates, made proclamation to that effect on the 3d day of June, 1813, and appointed the first Monday in July following for the meeting of the general assembly. Before the meeting of the legislature, Gen. William Clarke, the companion of Captain Lewis on the great exploring expedition, had been appointed by President Madison Governor of the Territory of Missouri and had entered on the discharge of the duties of the office. On the assembling of the legislature they passed such laws as were deemed indispensable, such as regulating weights and measures, the office and duties of sheriff, mode of taking the census, fixing the seats of justice in the counties, and their boundaries, the compensation to officers, establishing courts, and defining crimes and punishments, and incorporated the Bank of St. Louis. The territory was at that time divided into five counties, viz.: St. Charles, St. Louis, Ste. Genevieve, Cape Girardeau and New Madrid. At that session a portion of Ste. Genevieve was formed into Washington county. General William Clarke, who was well acquainted with the Missouri Indians, had immediately after the battle of Tippecanoe formed the resolution of collecting the prominent chiefs of the influential tribes who inhabited the regions of the Missouri, and taking them to Washington City and holding a council there with the President, and showing them the strength and, as far as possible, the wealth of the United States, to counteract the machinations of Tecumseh and his confederates.

With the approbation of the President and assistance of all the Missouri fur traders, he had collected at St. Louis, early in May, 1812, the chiefs of the Great and Little Osages, the Sacs, Renards, Delawares and Shawnees, to accompany him to Washington.

He was the brother of Gen. George Rogers Clarke, the hero of the West in the days of the Revolution, and was the compeer of Capt. Lewis in the expedition to the source of the Missouri and Columbia.

He was feared and beloved by the Indians. He understood their character almost by intuition, and could foresee their plans and intentions, and was their constant friend and protector from the impositions of white men. When they were all assembled preparatory to leaving on their long journey, their mutual friend advised them to make peace with each other, which they accordingly did for themselves and their respective people, and all buried the hatchet and left their friends at home in peace with all their neighbors.

On the following day, May the 5th, 1812, Gen. Clarke departed with all the chiefs of those powerful tribes, each preserving in their features and attire some peculiarity or custom of their particular tribe or nation.

More than half a century has since transpired, and probably every person engaged in that embassy of six nations is dead, but that act of Gen. Clarke alone should make his name immortal. Those six nations still exist and have kept their people on terms of friendship with each other to this late day. The object of the embassy was fully accomplished. The Indians arrived at Washington city several days before the declaration of war against Great Britain in 1812, and were presented to President Madison, who held a council and made a satisfactory treaty with them, after which they were shown through many large cities on their return to St. Louis, and escorted to their homes laden with many tokens of esteem and confidence, which are still preserved and shown to strangers as worthy of veneration and lasting preservation by all lovers of peace and friendship.

CHAPTER V.

Remarkable Performance of Col. Russell Farnum, a Fur Trader of St. Louis, Mo.

In the preceding chapters the brilliant achievements of many persons have been described and their biographies partially given, who, with patriotic zeal, in the moment of excitement, have stepped forward and jeopardized their lives and all they held dear in this world to rescue friends or punish enemies. It was a reward justly due them for their devotion and heroism, nor could a true history of St. Louis have been written without it.

In this chapter a single character and his family will form the theme, as it scarcely has a parallel in faithfulness, courage, perseverance and endurance in the annals of the world, and its omission here would mar its fulness and blur its most interesting pages. Col. Russell Farnum, a native of New Hampshire, had been a clerk for a time in the employment of John Jacob Astor, of New York, and was dispatched by him to visit his employes and agents in the Indian country of the West, and, with the aid of the late Wilson P. Hunt, to transact business as his agent, as his business and interests required. Farnum soon became well known in St. Louis, and at the commencement of the war of 1812 with Great Britain was on a business excursion in the Indian country near the Lake of the Woods.

Having finished his business in that distant region, and the leaves of autumn admonishing the near approach of winter, he essayed a return to St. Louis for winter quarters by the most feasible route at that time, and struck boldly across the forest from the lake toward the Mississippi at Prairie du Chien.

When he had reached the river, having heard nothing of the declaration of war, he saw a smoke at a distance and hastened to it. On his arrival at it he was immediately arrested by one of the wiseacres of that day, in the dress of a United officer in command of a barge and party of United States soldiers, and confined under close guard as a British spy until he arrived at St. Louis, where he was surrounded by a crowd of old friends who hurried him from the boat to his quarters before the officer could make his boat fast.

The officer was so mortified at this reception of his prisoner, and his own ill treatment of him while a prisoner—having seized on his journal—that he dared not show his face before him, but took his journal to the door of his lodgings and sent it in to him by one of the little daughters of Ham whom he met near the door of his lodgings. His stay in St. Louis was very brief. After consultation with his friends, Mr. Hunt and Gen. Clarke, Col. Farnum started alone with his dog and gun up the Missouri river to bear messages to the trading stations at and around Astoria, on the Pacific coast. The exact date of his departure and arrival at the different points of his long journey were carefully noted by him, as well as the remarkable incidents and observations on the route, in a well kept journal, prepared for publication, and was placed in the hands of a publisher in New York, who failed and died several years before Col. Farnum, and he was never after able to recover the journal or learn its fate.

His biographer is, therefore, obliged to rely on tradition, his own knowledge and the public journals of those days for the approximate dates and periods. Col. Farnum pursued the route traveled by Lewis and Clarke as much as possible, after passing the settlements, the last of which were near Boonville, on the Missouri river. His whole outfit, documents and blanket, except his gun, weighed less than twenty pounds, while he was a stout, athletic man, five feet ten inches high, of florid complexion, blue eyes and fair hair, of a happy and jovial disposition, and commanding countenance.

He had always been very temperate and healthy, and his long journey before him was not to subject him to labors to which he was a stranger or a diet to which he was not used. Game was plentiful; he was in his element; saw no enemies, for his trained dog would give notice of their presence in time to avoid them. He, therefore, traveled rapidly, without detention and without fear. The hostile Blackfeet Indians lay in his route; but he slept by day and traveled by night through their country, and passed unmolested and unobserved.

Obstacles now that no darkness could hide or foresight avoid presented a feature calculated to appal the bravest heart. The winter had set in; the earth covered with snow and the rivers with ice, while every track made by the traveler was visible to a roving enemy, whether man or beast; no succor near or sympathizer to soothe but his faithful dog; yet he pressed onward with speed. Every step took him further from friends and increased the ruggedness of his journey. His gun his only reliance for food for himself and companion; the caves and cliffs his only bed chamber by night and protection from storms and tempests by day. His costume corresponded with the length of his journey and the rudeness of his mode of life. A fur cap, a buckskin suit, with leggins and moccasins, formed his whole apparel, which was so similiar to an Indian's appearance at a distance that even the wild beasts allowed him passage without notice, and crossed his course within a few yards of him as one of their familiar sights.

His course was on the ice where the waters were frozen, and along the banks when open, as in the bluffs along nearly the whole course of the Missouri were found caves, recesses and overhanging rocks that afforded him shelter for the long, cold nights, and protection from the storms of a long, cold and tempestuous winter. The elks, black-tailed deer and mountain sheep roved in sufficient numbers, gnawing the moss from the rocks, to afford abundant food without the least trouble in searching for it, even in the snow storms of a week's duration by which he was detained.

Having at length overcome the great barrier between the oceans, he reached the waters of the Columbia, and leaving the inbound rivers behind, meditated taking a more easy and speedy mode of traveling to complete his journey. But while he sat on a log near the river, meditating the best means of accomplishing his object, his dog, lying at a little distance, jumped up, and running between his legs, manifested great alarm, when Col. Farnum, turning his eyes to the river, saw five canoes filled with Indians glide by like an arrow. Their hostile appearance, perfect outfit and celerity in motion at once determined him to pursue his journey in the same safe and humble manner in which he had performed the most difficult and dangerous part of it in safety, and, in pursuance of this resolution, he reached Astoria in perfect health, and delivered his dispatches in safety. When Col. Farnum had sufficiently recuperated to justify a further effort, he undertook the overland journey to St. Petersburgh, in Russia, and taking with him documents for the Hudson Bay Company, he walked up the Pacific coast to Kamskatka, still carrying his gun and accompanied by his dog, and arrived at the Behrings Strait in the winter of 1813-14, when it was frozen, and crossed it on the ice.

Then entering Siberia, he proceeded across the eastern continent to St. Petersburg, where, introducing himself to the American Plenipotentiary at the Russian Court, he was presented to the Emperor Alexander, as the bold American who had traveled by land across both continents. He was received by the Emperor with great consideration and kindness, and was sent by him, without solicitation, to Paris, on his way homeward, at which he arrived in good health, after such great exposure to dangers, toils and sufferings, *alone*, as no other individual has ever voluntarily submitted himself to on these two continents. On his appearance on the streets of St. Louis he was every where hailed with the warmest salutations of joy, pleasure and admiration in the countenances of all who had ever known him or heard of his extraordinary exploits. These demonstrations were received with that modesty and humility which always characterize true greatness, and adds a never failing charm to the whole character of him who possesses it.

The close of the war with Great Britain, just at the period of his return, afforded him an opportunity to resume his occupation as a fur trader, as he left it in the year 1812, which he embraced, and continued in honor and quietude to the end of his earthly career.

In 1830, Col. Farnum married the second daughter of Mr. Charles Bosseron, who survived him but a few years, by whom he left an infant son, named Charles.

Col. Farnum was attacked with cholera while on business at Rock Island, in 1832, but soon recovered and returned to St. Louis, where he died very suddenly soon after of the same disease. His only son, Charles, survived his father about eighteen years, and died of a pulmonary disease, leaving no one to inherit his father's name and fame, or enjoy his estate, but his aged maternal grandmother.

Thus passed away, in the morning of its day, one of the most promising families of St. Louis, surrounded with every blessing that could make life desirable, and with talents qualifying them to occupy a high place in the sphere of excellence and usefulness in the society in which they dwelt.

Disappointment and death, however, frustrated the labors of his life. First, the proposed publisher of his journal of travels failed and then died, by which it was lost. Then the derangement of the fur trade consequent upon the British war called for his whole attention in that direction for fifteen years after. Next, his marriage and domestic affairs left him no time to re-write, with care and accuracy, his own journal, and an inperfect work would never suit his taste.

His sudden death, therefore, has only left his friends to collect and publish the reminiscences of his extraordinary and wonderful journeys and the labors of his active life, without the aid of family connections, memoranda or data (except the public journals of the day) of any kind.

CHAPTER VI.

Reminiscences of Manuel Liza, a Spaniard, and his devotion to the United States in the War of 1812—The first Bank in St. Louis—Duel between Colonel Thomas H. Benton and Charles Lucas, Esq., and the result—The first Brick House in St. Louis—Missouri becomes a State of the Federal Union—The first Iron Foundry in St. Louis.

The last short chapter, although confined chiefly to the history of a single individual, furnishes a fair sample of what was daily being transacted at many places by a large number of the most enterprising people engaged in the fur trade on the waters of the Missouri. The most remarkable and enterprising among those who had chosen St. Louis for a residence was Manuel Liza, a Spaniard by birth, but long a sojourner and trader among the Indians on the Missouri. His known popularity among the Indians induced Gen. Clark to appoint him a sub-agent among the Indians of the Missouri in 1814, while the war against Great Britain and the Indians of the Great Lakes and Mississippi was in progress. He accepted the appointment, and taking a supply of suitable merchandise for the purpose, furnished by the United States, distributed them among the Indians of the Missouri, and engaged them in offensive operations against the enemies of the United States. His trading posts extended at that time twelve hundred miles up the Missouri river, therefore he could select those best qualified for that service, and accordingly made choice of the Yanktons and Omahas for that purpose, and distributed the goods among them. The Omahas lost no time in delay, but made a successful raid on the hostile Iowas, allies of the enemy, took several of their scalps and sent them to St. Louis, in the month of February, 1815, before the news of peace had reached them. In the meantime, Mr. Liza had collected nine hundred Yanktons at the mouth of the Rio Jacques, who also attacked the Iowas, took twenty-seven of their scalps and were preparing to drive the whole tribe from the lands of their fathers, the last chastisement of a native among Indians, when the news of peace was received, and a request from Gen. Howard to bring down forty-seven of the warrior chiefs to St. Louis. This he accomplished with ease, as his character among Indians was held in the highest estimation, and his counsels followed. His position and influence brought upon him the envy and opposition of those in the same business, who attacked him in the public journals and vexed him into a resignation after he had filled the office three years with the most consummate skill and perfect satisfaction to the Indian Department. His active and eventful life, his palatial residence of that day, his remarkable Indian acquaintance and his popularity, his two marriages, his very extensive fur trading establishment, and his character for probity and honor point him out as one of the great builders of the fame of St. Louis, and furnish suitable excuse for giving his name and actions a place in its history, as he left no sons or near relatives to inherit his fame or his name, and half a century has nearly obliterated the memory of his competitors and traducers of that day. The close of the war had opened a greater competition among the Missouri fur traders, and new parties had come into the field to participate in it, so that on the death of Mr. Liza no considerable vacuum occurred in the trade, notwithstanding his death and absence from the vast field of his labors. The labors of the trade were gradually undergoing a change. Hunters and trappers were to be employed as well as clerks, traps and toils, as well as goods credited to the Indians, and all transported to greater distances, as the game and Indians both gradually retired before the advance of civilization, which was making advances into the wilderness with most gigantic strides. Such was the state of the fur trade in the regions of the Missouri for many years after the British war—even to this day. The new adventurers who came into Missouri as the fur trade receded, brought forward new schemes of finance, and, engaging the old, experienced traders and substantial citizens of the village in the enterprise, on the 21st day of August, 1816, obtained a charter for a bank from the Territorial Legislature, to be located in St. Louis, by the name of the St. Louis Bank. On the 2d of September, 1816, thirteen directors were elected, who chose Colonel Samuel Hammond, President, and John G. B. Smith, Cashier, and the bank soon went into operation. The little town felt new life. The current of business swelled in volume and increased in velocity from the flood of money. The people, elated by this new apparent progress in the road to wealth, on the first of February, 1817, obtained another charter for a bank, with a capital of $250,000, called the Bank of Missouri, which was soon after made the depository of the money of the United States, Auguste Chouteau being chosen President, and Lilburn W. Boggs, Cashier, of the elected directory.

The tide of business was thus inflated by the flood of money to an excessive magnitude and extravagance encouraged, while speculation, encouraged by banking facilities, jeopardized everything by the momentum it gave to all financial transactions. Immigration flowed into the Territory from all the States in a most rapid current, attracted hither by three great objects—the speedy acquisition of wealth, good lands at low prices, and large tracts for hemp and tobacco plantations, to be cultivated by slaves. When all these were at the zenith of action the United States held sales of the public lands for the first time in Missouri, at which great numbers of speculators congregated and added to the general enthusiasm and scramble for wealth and power.

In this glittering season irresponsible and reckless persons obtained credit of the banks and soon involved them in insolvency, and many of the officers in disgrace and ruin. In this season of hope and folly many enterprises were undertaken and much labor and funds expended on edifices in the city of St. Louis which were never completed. Such were two brick church buildings on Market street—one a Catholic church near the southwest corner of Second and Market streets, one hundred and thirty feet long, and the other a Baptist church, at the southwest corner of Third and Market streets. Both were inclosed and used many years by those who erected them, and finally demolished before they were finished. Also the foundation of a large theater was laid on the south side of Chesnut street, between Second and Third streets, where the Police Court is now held, which was never used. This financial crash and disappointment was not confined to the people of St. Louis and Missouri. The whole United States suffered alike at the period. Insolvency was a term well understood out of Missouri as well as in it. Her exports were only lead, furs and peltries up to that time, and were but little affected in price by the general stagnation and crash. The great drain on Missouri was through the land offices to pay for homesteads at two dollars per acre which are now donated to all actual settlers. That was a sad burden, then and has been one of the great unacknowledged errors of our departed rulers. The overtasking early settlers of Western States has been more felt in the payments for homesteads than in taxation for all other purposes and the burden of military service in all the wars. Speculators have been tolerated and encouraged, while the toiling settlers have opened the roads, built the bridges, fought the battles and paid the taxes. Speculators' lands were always exempt by law five years. Money appearing very plentiful in St. Louis in the spring of 1817, many persons essayed to provide themselves with more comfortable residences than they had enjoyed before, and many new buildings were erected and occupied during this year, which seemed one of unusual prosperity. The year, however, was marked by an occurrence which created much excitement at the time by its tragical termination, and requires to be noted by the historian, as it occurred between two distinguished individuals, who each occupied the front rank of the two political parties of that day.

Mr. Charles Lucas, then United States Attorney for the Territory of Missouri, and Colonel Thomas H. Benton, afterwards United States Senator for thirty consecutive years, were engaged in the trial of a cause in court on opposite sides, and, forgetting the dignity of the court and the kindness and courtesy due to their brother members of the same honorable profession, in their zeal for their respective clients, used harsh and reproachful language to each other. Colonel Benton, considering himself insulted by Mr. Lucas, sent a challenge which Mr. Lucas declined to accept on the basis that he was not to be held accountable for words spoken in professional debate. At a political meeting held soon after, the same gentlemen became much excited in the discussion of some controversy, and Mr. Lucas sent a challenge to Colonel Benton, which he accepted. On the 12th of August a meeting took place on Bloody Island, now a part of East St. Louis, to decide their difference with pistols, in which Mr. Lucas received a severe wound in the neck and was withdrawn from the field by his surgeon. At a subsequent meeting of the same parties, on the 27th of September, 1817, Mr. Lucas fell, aged twenty-five years, deeply lamented by a vast number of admiring friends and near relatives.

In the eagerness to raise capital even for praiseworthy objects in the maniacal year 1817, recourse was had to legislative authority to authorize lotteries, and so blind to wise policy and good morals was the legislative assembly at that time that they granted authority for three lotteries—one to create a fund to build an academy at Potosi; one to purchase fire engines for the town of St. Louis; and one for the erection of a Masonic Hall.

And, strange as it may appear in this enlightened age, while we are paying enormous sums for public schools, jails and penitentiaries, our legislature continues this sad reproach on the wisdom and morals of our rulers, and our streets are yet dishonored by the signs of Missouri State Lottery offices. Notwithstanding this blindness and folly in legislation, the same legislature incorporated the board of trustees for superintending the St. Louis public schools, which was the commencement of the public school system which is in operation at this day, and is the most noble and praiseworthy institution

St. Louis has to transmit to posterity. The selection of trustees for that important station gave it the high character as a board that it has ever since maintained, and showed that they had the interest of posterity in full view. They were Gen. William Clarke, William C. Carr, Thomas H. Benton, Bernard Pratte, Auguste Chouteau, Alexander McNair and John P. Cabanne. The high character of all these gentlemen and the important trust conferred on them by the legislature, together with the necessity of public schools in all communities, induced the belief that the public schools would then soon be opened by the board. A cruel disappointment, however, followed, and no public school was opened for twenty years afterwards for the education of the innumerable idle children of St. Louis. The census of the United States in 1810 gave 20,845 of all classes to Missouri, and in 1820 it gave 66,586. The first brick dwelling house in St. Louis was erected by William C. Carr, in 1813, and from that period all seemed to perceive that brick walls would be most suitable for all edifices to be erected on the site chosen for the city. More than half a century has now passed, and nine-tenths of the chief material of which they are manufactured is very abundant in and about St. Louis, of an excellent quality. The manufacture of brick, from its first introduction as a building material into St. Louis to the present time, has kept a more even pace with the growth of its population than the manufacture of any other article. None have ever been imported into the city or exported from it. They have always commanded a fair but never an exorbitant price, and from the abundance and excellence of the materials of which they are made in the vicinity, or near easy transportation to the city, there can be no doubt that St. Louis will always have the appearance of a city built chiefly of brick, however large may be its circumference. Grey limestone abounds in and about the vicinity of the city of an excellent quality, and large quantities of lime are exported from it to other places. The expense of building in St. Louis and its vicinity has been greater than in most other cities, in consequence of the high price of pine lumber, there being no pine forests within fifty miles of the city. Rents have, therefore, been higher, and it has retarded the manufacturing interest more than any other cause. During the exuberance of money in 1817, in the general scramble to acquire wealth, some learned, staid and scientific persons of other parts of the Union came to St. Louis and other parts of Missouri and essayed with the capital they brought with them to become opulent farmers, planters and landholders, and although they exercised industry, sobriety and prudence, failed by lack of patience, fortitude and perseverance.

One instance is but the example of many in Missouri about that time, and is given to contrast with some who patiently waited for the growth of the little town, and now bask on the bosom of wealth and behold the rising glory of St. Louis, surrounded by their families and friends who have assisted in extending its limits and enjoying its fruition. Col. Justus Post was, in 1817, one of the best informed and wealthiest citizens of the territory, had been educated at West Point, was a profound practical mathematician, and had served with credit in the United States army during the war of 1812 against Great Britain. He was possessed of an estate of one hundred thousand dollars, mostly cash, purchased large tracts of land, built a country residence and a mill in Bonhomme township, made other improvements and gave embellishment to the country and life to business about him. The stockholders of the Missouri Bank elected him a director in it and thereby involved him in an element he had but imperfectly studied. In extricating himself from its meshes he became impatient, discouraged and desirous of change in his location, and as the people of Illinois wished to employ a competent engineer to examine a route for the Michigan canal, he engaged himself to them, performed the task satisfactorily, left Missouri and settled in the little town called America, in Illinois, engaged again in milling and died poor, having disposed of his large land estate in St. Louis county for a trifle when he left, which, if held to his death, would have left his two sons millionaires.

The growth of St. Louis and the influx of emigrants to the territory during the year 1817 elated the whole population and urged them to attempt many projects in imitation of the more advanced society of older places. A Bible society was formed by the more prominent of the Protestant members of society, which was called the Missouri Auxiliary Bible Society, and continued to exist for many years. In the year 1818, Missouri applied for admission into the Union, having all the constitutional requisites for admission. The slavery question had begun to be agitated the year before in some of the Eastern States, and at once became a theme of great interest in all the States as soon as the application was made to Congress. The people of Missouri took a lively interest in the impending question and were much divided on the subject, but the preponderance was somewhat in favor of slavery.

The agitation was very exciting in Missouri and both in and out of Congress. Both parties became so much excited that the peace of the country was much endangered and the progress of improvement much impeded. This, with the failure of the St. Louis banks and the suspension of specie payments by the banks of most of the States, produced a stagnation in almost all kinds of business. Confidence among men of business was greatly impaired, the courts thronged with creditors striving to collect what might save themselves from impending ruin, the bulletin-boards of the court house were covered with advertisements of sheriff's sales, and the streets filled with idle men out of employment. Such was the condition of St. Louis in the days of the fierce agitation of the Missouri question. Emigration to the State was nearly suspended, while lands depreciated in value until they were scarcely saleable.

At length the Missouri Compromise, as it was called, was effected, and Missouri entered the Union, but with the incubus of slavery upon her, and with the certain prospect of being surrounded on three sides by free States, to tease and endanger the owners of slave property so much that they were held in lower estimation in Missouri than in any other State. The progress of improvement was thereby greatly impeded, and the public mind agitated by the threatening aspect of surrounding objects. Moreover, there was a large party at the formation of the Constitution who were opposed to its becoming a slave State, and very reluctantly submitted to the evils of slavery brought upon them, one of which was the depreciation in the price of real estate, by stopping emigration from the Northern States to it. The improvement in navigation by steamboat had now come to be known and appreciated, but its progress was very slow in consequence of the timidity of St. Louis capitalists to invest in steamboats. When Missouri was admitted into the Union there was no steamboat owned in the State, and but one steam mill; consequently other States enjoyed the carrying trade, which had become large and lucrative on the Mississippi, below St. Louis. The transportation above the town was still continued in barges, as in former times. The town was governed by a board of five Trustees, elected annually by the people, who appointed a register to write out their ordinances and see that they were enforced. They also appointed an assessor and an inspector of lumber. These constituted the officers of the corporation, and performed all the business. The assessed amount of taxable property was less than one million of dollars, and the whole corporation tax less than four thousand dollars per annum, while Missouri remained a territory.

The boundary of the taxable portion of the Territory, under the corporation of 1809 (when it was formed), began at the mouth of Mill Creek, near the site of the gas works, thence up the creek westwardly to about Seventh street, thence northwardly with Seventh street to Green street, thence on the north line of Green street to the middle of the Mississippi, thence southwardly by the river to the place of beginning, having seven streets parallel with the river. The streets were very limited in breadth, as first surveyed by the French and Spanish authorities, as the town was to be fortified. Therefore, all the streets that were laid off within the old fortifications, that is east of Fourth street, are still narrow, while all west of Third street are much broader, being sixty or eighty feet wide. The cross streets within the old fortifications are similar to the parallel streets, being scarcely forty feet wide, while those outside of Fourth street are broad and convenient. The blocks thus formed were larger in the older part of the town than the new, by the difference in the breadth of the streets, and were about three hundred feet square in the original survey. At the time of the adoption of the constitution of the State—1820 —which may be assumed as an epoch (although it was not admitted into the Union until the next year), the town contained six hundred houses, one-third of which were of stone or brick, the remainder wooden, one-half of which were framed. The population was estimated at 5,000, one fourth of whom were French families, the remainder mostly emigrants from the other United States and foreigners from all parts of Europe. The fur companies were extending their establishments still further up the Missouri river and its branches, although all other business was exceedingly dull, by reason of the failure of the banks. The estimated annual value of the trade was $600,000.

The failure of the banks and the oppression of debtors by their creditors induced the Legislature at its first session to enact a stay-law for the relief of debtors, which protected their property from distraint for two years and a half, and also established a system of loan offices, and issued a paper currency that soon lost the public confidence and became of little benefit to the public when it did answer the purpose of canceling debts or purchasing property, as it was of very uncertain value by reason of speculators depreciating its value that they might purchase it for a small consideration. Notwithstanding these disadvantages, the town and State advanced in population and wealth. Two ferries with boats, propelled by horse-power, became necessary to accommodate the emigrants and traveling public at St. Louis.

Steamboats from the Ohio river assumed the carrying trade of that river, and from New Orleans to St. Louis, so that keel-boating was nearly discontinued on the streams below the town, and the arrival and departure of a steamboat became a common occurence. The imports were estimated at one million of dollars in 1820, as but few articles, and those of the most simple kind, had as yet been manufactured in the State; the balance of trade was therefore much against the new State, which was without capitalists or credit. There was, however, no lack of enterprise among the people; and among those of that early day who should be remembered as one of St. Louis' early benefactors was Lewis Newell, a blacksmith, who established the first foundry of iron in the city of St. Louis in 1824, and operated it in connection with his own trade, and then added the manufacturing of plows to his extensive establishment, assisted by Mr. Schroeder, who still manufactures plows on Second street, near the old site of Newell's foundry.

CHAPTER VII.

The Incorporation of the town of St. Louis by the Legislature, with a Charter for a City—The Expedition of Gen. William H. Ashley to the Rocky Mountains, and his Defeat by Auricaree Indians on the Missouri—Duel between Thos. C. Rector and Joshua Barton, in which the latter was killed.

The gradual disappearance of depreciated paper money from commercial circles and returning prosperity through industrial pursuits had begun to show itself early in the spring of 1822. Specie had taken the place of paper in nearly all commercial transactions, and consisted almost exclusively of silver coin, mostly Spanish or Mexican dollars. The exports being very limited, most of it had been brought and put in circulation by emigrants, as no amount of payments were then made in American gold, in consequence of the United States golden dollar being more valuable than a silver one by several cents, which gave rise to Senator Benton's *gold bill*, so celebrated at a later day throughout the United States.

The stay law in the meantime had the effect to prevent great sacrifices of property by sheriff's sales, and many compromises were made during the stay that greatly relieved the debtors in many instances. Still, however, the courts were crowded with creditors pressing their claims into judgment for future action on the termination of the stay law. Agriculture had begun to receive greater attention as the population increased, many of the emigrants from the Southern States having brought their slaves to Missouri with the design of cultivating tobacco and hemp.

An agricultural society was formed in May of this year, and embraced among its distinguished members, Hon. Wm. C. Carr, Major Richard Graham, Dr. Robert Simpson, Colonel Joseph C. Brown, and others. It did much for the advancement of agriculture for many years.

The Legislature of Missouri, on the 9th day of December, 1822, passed an act to incorporate the inhabitants of the town of St. Louis into the city of St. Louis, and vested the corporate powers in a Mayor and nine Aldermen. The town of St. Louis then contained 4,800 inhabitants. On the first Monday in April, 1823, an election was held for a Mayor and nine Aldermen, which resulted as follows:

Dr. Wm. Carr Lane was elected Mayor, and Thos. McKnight, James Kennerly, Philip Rocheblave, Archibald Gamble, Wm. H. Savage, Robert Nash, James Loper, Henry Von Phul and James Lackman, were elected Aldermen.

These officers were gentlemen of the first respectability, and entered on the discharge of their duties with the entire confidence of the people in their integrity and ability.

The city was divided into three wards, the northern, the southern and the middle, and preparations made to improve the city. Some attempts had previously been made to pave some of the streets, but the designs had not been accomplished as originally contemplated, and were then suspended. The new government, immediately after its organization, caused its engineer to submit a plan for the grading and paving of the city, and, as contemplated, he commenced his labors at the most important point in it, and submitted a grade for Main street, from near the Iron Mountain Depot on the south, to the intersection of Green street on the north.

This grade was adopted by ordinance, and the grading and paving between Market and Walnut streets completed in the autumn of that year.

The grading was done at the cost of the city, but the paving and curbing was done at the cost of the owners of lots fronting on the streets paved. This was the cause of many of the owners of large lots dividing and selling them and thus affording an opportunity for the improvement of the city in its central parts where the town had long been disfigured or hidden by rustic and nearly useless inclosures to gratify the whim of some antiquated occupant in possession.

While these operations were in progress, and improvements advancing apace in all parts of the State, the veterans in the fur trade were not idle, but forming new schemes and making new efforts to extend their traffic and establishments further into the regions of the West.

Among all those who have distinguished themselves by their enterprise, perseverance and success no one has excelled the late Gen. William H. Ashley, the intrepid leader and head of the Rocky Mountain Fur Company of St. Louis.

He it was who discovered the great Southern pass of that mighty barrier, the Rocky Mountains, and published to the world the extent and productions of those distant and unexplored solitudes, which, by their vastness and minerals, attract the cupidity of millions at this time.

It may at first view appear a digression from our history to mention him, but any part of his history is a part of the history of St. Louis and Missouri, and can not be omitted in their history. Early in the spring of this year Gen. Ashley equipped two boats of suitable capacity and strength to ascend the Missouri river to the mouth of the Yellowstone river, and with the assistance of Major Henry, an experienced fur trader, engaged one hundred men to accompany and navigate the two boats and perform such other service as is usually required of men in the service of fur companies engaged in trade with the Indians.

These were mostly Missourians, long experienced in the hardships of trading expeditions on the Missouri among the Indians, and many were natives of St. Louis.

The Rocky Mountain Fur Company had provided a complete assortment of Indian goods for an extensive and lucrative traffic, and no expedition of the same size could then have been better furnished in St. Louis. The goods and most of the men being embarked as early as the season would permit, the two boats left the town amid hilarity and expressions of good will and wishes from many mouths. Alas! how mutable are human affairs, and how subject our fondest hopes to be frustrated! No want of prudence, foresight or sagacity on the part of Gen. Ashley was ever imputed to him in the disasters and disappointments he sustained within the next three months, by which he lost more than one-fourth of his men by violent deaths, and one-half of his property by accident, deceit or war. First, a cart-load of rifle powder on its way to the boats at St. Charles exploded on Washington avenue, near where the St. Louis University now stands, and killed two of his men and Mr. LaBarge, owner and driver of the cart.

Next, the chiefs of the Auricaree Indians, by deceit, obtained a valuable lot of presents for their friendship, after which they sold him fifty horses and obtained full payment; and to complete their perfidy attacked his men on the very ground appointed for the delivery of the horses and killed fifteen of his men, wounded others, shot, wounded and dispersed the horses, and closed their villainy by driving his boats from their anchorage down the river, and effectually blockaded the stream against him.

While these disasters were occurring in his immediate presence, a party of eleven of his men was attacked near the mouth of the Yellowstone river, whither he had sent Major Henry by land with a small detachment, and four more of his most efficient men were slain and the whole property in their charge taken from them by the Blackfoot Indians.

This series of misfortunes, that would have appalled and quite discouraged other men, had no perceptible effect on the countenance or energy of Gen. Ashley. His mild, peaceful and grave countenance underwent no change, nor his plans or purposes any alteration.

He bided his time for action with the quietude and patience of a cat waiting for the appearance of its prey, and was rewarded for his silence in much the same manner.

The traders of the Hudson Bay Fur Company had prompted these raids on his property, and when the United States army had chastised the Auricarees and dissolved the blockade of the Missouri river, he proceeded to his establishment at the mouth of the Yellowstone, and, securing his boats and other property from the danger of further depredations, went immediately in pursuit of his plundered property among the Hudson Bay Fur Company traders and their Indian dupes whom enticed into these murders and maraudings. His promptitude was rewarded with complete success; and, while in pursuit of a squad of trans-mountain Indians, he was led into the gateway of the great Southern Pass, and the direct road to the fruition of all his hopes for wealth, honor and rewards—for all his patient labors, exposures, meditations, watchings, disappointments and waitings among the mutations and dangers of his adventurous life. Having secured complete success for himself and partners, he quietly and almost unnoticed returned to St. Louis and purchased a beautiful site for a residence near the Old Reservoir, and expended a portion of his hard-earned wealth in building up and beautifying the city and his tranquil home.

The smooth stream of human affairs is sometimes very suddenly disturbed by very small and unlooked for circumstances, and society shocked and excited by its action and consequences. Such an occurrence transpired in St. Louis in June of this year. Gen. William Rector, United States Surveyor of Illinois, Missouri and Arkansas, was absent from the city in Washington City, on official business connected with his office, when an article appeared in the Missouri *Republican* charging him with corruption in office. It was a charge too serious to be overlooked. His brother, Thomas C. Rector, immediately called on the editor for the name of the author. The editor gave the name of Joshua Barton, Esq., United States District Attorney and brother of Hon. David Barton, United States Senator of Missouri, as the author. Mr. Rector and Mr. Barton were gentlemen of high respectability. The code of honor that obtained in the West at that time could not be misunderstood or evaded. Mr. Rector challenged Mr. Barton, who accepted the challenge, and they met on Bloody Island, June 30, 1823. Mr. Barton fell at the first fire, and died lamented by a large number of admiring friends.

The public excitement from the bloody incidents on the Missouri and in St. Louis already related had begun to be quieted and hopes of more peaceful times to attend its distant citizens engaged in the lucrative and extended Western fur trade, when the public ear was again shocked by the recital of new atrocities committed by the Indians of Upper Missouri on the citizens of St. Louis, by which several prominent persons lost their lives and others their property.

The Missouri Fur Company was one of the strongest and most active companies engaged in the trade, and had Dr. Pilcher, a most distinguished Indian fur trader, at its head. Maj. Benj. O'Fallon was one of the principal partners and at the same time one of the most efficient United States agents for Indian Affairs. Dr. Pilcher, however, had the whole management of the company's affairs. In conducting its affairs he engaged two of the most expert and experienced men of that day to assist him, named Jones and Jemmell.

These two gentlemen were sent forward by Dr. Pilcher in

command of a party carrying fifteen thousand dollars worth of goods to the company's store-house near the mouth of the Yellowstone river, and, when near the end of their journey, they were attacked in a defile by about four hundred Blackfoot Indians, and both the leaders and five others of the party slain and all the property taken. Each of the leaders made a desperate defense and were cut to pieces. Jones killed two Indians, and Jemmell one before they perished. These murders were afterwards avenged, which was but a lean and unsatisfactory consolation to bereaved relatives, friends and plundered merchants.

CHAPTER VIII.

The First Female Charitable Society Formed in St. Louis—Return of Gen. Ashley, Successful, from the Rocky Mountains—Election of Hon. Frederick Bates, Governor, and his Early Death.

Gov. Alexander McNair's term of office was now drawing to a close in 1824. It had been an entire success, and he retired from its duties with the gratifying consciousness that his entire administration had given satisfaction to the people in all parts of the State, and his example was worthy of imitation. Indeed, his official career was always a success in all stations. He had filled many offices, both civil and military, in the Territorial, State and Indian departments with credit to himself and satisfaction to the public. He owed but little to scientific training or brilliant abilities, but he possessed a sound judgment, an honest heart and patriotic purpose, from which no allurements could ever divert him. His house was the abode of hospitality and the high school of refinement in St. Louis and Missouri, and people from all parts of the State resorted to it as to the home of a brother and were received by his accomplished wife with the affection of a sister or a mother and made welcome to all it afforded. Information was sought and given there by politicians of all parties with the utmost freedom and kind feelings, for peace and wisdom always presided there in the person of Mrs. McNair and her well-trained children. St. Louis was singularly favored many consecutive years by the presence of the presiding Executive officers of the Territory and State and their exemplary families, for what has been written of Gov. McNair and family applies as well to his predecessor, Gov. William Clarke, and family. Both families were held in the highest estimation as fit examples to all others.

The first Female Charitable Society of St. Louis was organized at the house of Gov. McNair, in the early part of this year, and Mrs. George F. Strother was elected the first President and Mrs. McNair was elected first Vice-President of the society, composed of the most respectable ladies of all creeds.

It was the first charitable society organized in St. Louis, and continued its operations, affording great relief to the poor, until the growth of the city rendered more efficient charitable associations indispensable.

The military operations of the United States against the hostile tribes of Indians of the Upper Missouri attracted the notice of all the peaceful tribes, and caused them to desire a personal interview with Gen. Clarke, the Indian Agent, and beloved and revered friend of all red men, now grown too old to visit them at their distant homes. Therefore a few of the prominent men of almost every peaceful tribe visited General Clarke with their families, dressed and painted in the most fanciful and varied styles of their different nations, during the summer, and were received by the General in the most dignified manner in his council chamber, which was his museum—a large room hung and filled in all parts with Indian curiosities alone: canoes, oars, arms, coats of mail, shields, clothes, beds, ornaments of every kind, cooking utensils, pipes, knives, spoons, trays, dishes, agricultural, mechanical and musical instruments, snow shoes and feet coverings, men and women's head gear, infants' clothing and cradles. They all came by their own conveyance and returned in the same way, in canoes, and while here encamped on the river bank between Green street and Bremen, then occupied by but five houses.

The Indians, while visiting St. Louis, were in the habit of dressing themselves immediately after breakfast (which they always cooked themselves from provisions furnished by General Clarke) in their best attire, and then spent the day in a single group going from house to house showing themselves and dancing, singing, or making rude music in the style of their country, to amuse their auditory, some of whom would commonly make them a donation, and if it was liberal or several of them made, the performance was at once encored; but if nothing was contributed, or some rude boy spat upon a dancer's foot or leg, the music ceased and the performers sullenly marched out of sight before they essayed further performances.

These friendly visits and primitive exhibitions continued during the lifetime of Gen. Clarke, since which they have entirely ceased, and it would now be a novel sight to view a similar group walking through the streets of St. Louis, and attract as much attention as a herd of camels, so rapidly have the Indians since that period retired and given place to civilization and improvement. In June of this year the hearts of many in the city and throughout the State were gladdened by the return of the survivors of Gen. Ashley's Rocky Mountaineers, after an absence of fifteen months through the most arduous, dangerous and interesting scenes that it is possible for men to be hired or persuaded into, and after having accomplished more for themselves, their employers and their country, than any person had dreamed of or thought possible to accomplish. They had enriched their employers, destroyed the influence of the Hudson Bay Fur Company among the Indians, and expelled their traders from the country. They had discovered an easy and practicable passage through the Rocky Mountains and examined the unexplored solitudes and vastly rich mineral regions beyond them, and laid them open to commerce and future cultivation. They had received double pay for their labors, and had assisted in avenging their fallen friends and secured safety from future aggression.

It was no fiction. The demonstration was with them in the form of innumerable packs of beaver skins and other valuable furs and peltries that crowded the safely returned boats to St. Louis.

Their leader was here, unchanged and unchangeable in countenance or action. Still as an oyster, but vigilant as Argus, forming new schemes corresponding with the advancing progress of the age. He served as Lieutenant Governor during the term of Gov. McNair. A general election was to be held in August for all State officers and a member of Congress, the State having but one representative by the appointment of 1820, at that time.

In the political movements of the day there seemed to be a great variety of sentiment, and many candidates were presented by their respective friends for almost every office. The election was held on the first Monday in August, at which Gen. William H. Ashley and Frederick Bates were candidates for Governor, the latter of whom was elected, but served only a small portion of his term, and died suddenly on the first of August following, of pleurisy.

At this election John K. Walker was elected sheriff of St. Louis county, and being re-elected at the end of his term, filled that office four years. Hon. John Scott was re-elected to Congress for another term, having represented Missouri from the time of its admission into the Union, and as a delegate while it was a territory. As there were then several persons in nomination for the Presidency of the United States, four of whom were quite prominent, the probability was even thus early in the canvass that there would be no election in the electoral college, and that the election would ultimately be in the House of Representatives, in which case Missouri would be more certain of strength than New York or any large State whose Representatives might be divided. Therefore, the vote for Congressmen was most carefully watched by all the four parties, viz.: Adams, Clay, Crawford and Jackson, each of whom hoped Mr. Scott would favor them; hence his easy triumph over all competitors.

While political affairs engrossed the attention of a few politicians, the great body of Missourians were more profitably engaged in preparing for the rising greatness of the State.

Every laborer in the rural districts (and indeed all was rural then), was striving to add his might to the general improvement and productiveness of the country, and it is now wonderful what a beneficial and happy effect that general action in one direction produced at that time. Good wheat was plentiful at 50 cents per bushel, corn 20 cents, potatoes the same, flour $1 50 per cwt., corn meal half that price. Corn fed, dressed pork, 1 50 per cwt., by the wagon load; beef at the same price. Cows with young calves at from eight to twelve dollars, and good work oxen at from thirty to forty dollars per pair. Strange as it may now appear, people were soon out of debt and required no banks or loan offices for their relief or accommodation. New fences, new fields and new dwellings were rising in all directions and immigrants entering the State at every avenue. The older settlers who had involved themselves in debt during the banking mania having recovered their reason, sold out their improved estates to the new comers, paid their debts and commenced business anew, wiser if not better men than before.

These were halycon days to Missouri. Everything seemed growing new and young. There were no bank runners then hurrying about town, distributing little bits of paper marked with "Your note for $—, due on —," rendering the nights of the receiver feverish, sleepless and suicidal, and his visits to customers early next day uninvited and unpleasant.

The nights of spring and autumn were mostly nights of illuminations in one direction or another, as large prairies abounded in both the States of Missouri and Illinois, and the plowman had not controlled and prevented their annual burnings as at this day. Following every pleasant day of the spring and autumn of 1824 the heavens were illuminated on one side or the other, and sometimes nearly all round from the horizon to near the zenith by accident or design, and having passed control, often blazed during the whole night with most astonishing brilliancy, illuminating nearly the whole hemisphere. It was very common then on those brilliant occasions for large groups of people to assemble on the Big Mound, Iron Mountain and Pilot Knob to view the grandeur of the scene, than which few are more fascinating and sublime in all the works of nature or art. These, however, have forever passed away in the rapid march of improvement and the ever changing panorama of human affairs, and we are left with but a feeble description of those common, grand and sublime exhibitions of nature, interest and accidents of those early days in Missouri and Illinois.

The result of the State election in August had developed the fact that Henry Clay was the first choice of the great body of the people for the Presidency, and he received the undivided presidential votes of the State in the college of Missouri, and forty-one electoral votes for President in the United States.

This, with his acknowledged ability and great popularity, flattered the people of Missouri that their favorite would be elected in the House of Representatives, since the election would end there.

This hope was strengthened by the re-election of Hon. David Barton to the Senate of the United States on the 25th of November, 1824, for six years, where his influence was expected in favor of Mr. Clay among his friends in the House of Representatives. Hon. John Scott had received 5,031 votes for Congressman at the State election in August; Hon. George F. Strother, who had once represented a district of Virginia, received 4,528, and Hon. Robert Wash 1,125 votes. In all the votes given for these respective candidates not one was cast with the view, hope or intention that it should aid in electing John Quincy Adams to the Presidency of the United States over Henry Clay, the favorite and friend of Missouri, or the Southern hero, Andrew Jackson, who had received four more votes than any other candidate in the electoral college. Andrew Jackson had received 87 votes, John Quincy Adams 83, Henry Clay 41, including 3 from Missouri, and Mr. Crawford 30 votes in the college.

Missouri was a slave State and supposed to be in sympathy with the other slave States and those bordering on the Ohio and its tributaries, and had so shown herself by her electoral votes. Twenty-five States then formed the Federal Union and thirteen were necessary to a choice. Well informed people throughout the United States supposed they knew from the voice of the people how their servants, the Representatives, would vote; that is, they had every evidence that is usually relied on that on the first ballot Adams would receive 12 votes, Jackson 7 votes, Crawford 4 votes, and Clay 1 vote, necessitating a second ballot at least.

The appointed day at length arrived, and many came prepared to witness a long and honorable struggle, but saw only a prescribed routine pursued in silence during a short period, when the announcement of the first ballot was made, and John Quincy Adams declared duly elected President of the United

States, receiving the votes of thirteen States; Andrew Jackson 8, Mr. Crawford 4, and Henry Clay none. It was evident at a glance that Missouri's representative had disappointed her expectations, and had seized on the pillars of the temple of hope for any of the other candidates, and pulled down the whole fabric, and buried his political life beyond the power of resurrection in Missouri in the debris of down-fallen political faith.

Gratitude to Mr. Clay for his services to Missouri left him still many friends, but the growing popularity of Gen. Jackson soon pointed him out as the available candidate for the next presidency, and Mr. Clay's friends mostly attached themselves to his party as did also Mr. Crawford's.

This movement gave Missouri a broad and stable front in the line of the friends of General Jackson, and they took the chief responsibility of political affairs for many years thereafter.

CHAPTER IX.

The Invitation to the Marquis de LaFayette to Visit St. Louis, and his Acceptance—His Arrival, Reception and Departure.

The disappointment of Missouri by the action of their representative in the presidential election was borne with philosophic patience and a watchful eye kept on all desirable vacancies within reach of a presidential gift as a reward for the presidential vote of Missouri.

Nothing criminal or unseemly in the premises, however, was ever developed. He had joined himself to his idol and was permitted to worship it without opposition by all disappointed constituents. Missouri was not without strength and respectability in Congress, notwithstanding the defection of its only representative.

She had two giants in the Senate in the persons of Hon. Thomas H. Benton and Hon. David Barton, than whom two more able men seldom if ever graced the American Senate. They did not always entertain the same views on national measures, but they could explain their views in the most lucid manner that language can present, and, as the character of each for sincerity was never doubted, their words always carried weight, if not conviction, to the judgment of their hearers and always gave them a crowded and attentive auditory and merited fame.

The city of St. Louis had enjoyed the advantage of its chartered rights under its indefatigable and accomplished Mayor, Dr. William Carr Lane, two years, and had adopted a system of street improvements that gave evidence of a determination on the part of the people to make it a commercial and manufacturing city with all the advantages the Mississippi could be made to afford.

The attempt, therefore, of Dr. Lane to retire from the Mayoralty, in the spring of 1825, would not be listened to by the people, and he was re-elected each succeeding year, as if by acclamation, as long as he could be persuaded to fill the office.

Front street, or the Levee as it is now called, then had no existence as a street or landing, except at the east end of a few cross streets, but was a serrated limestone ledge of rocks, which formed a part of the inclosures of the blocks east of First or Main street, from the north line of the city to near the foot of Spruce street, where it disappeared under the alluvial bottom of Mill Creek, the southern boundary of the city at that period. The formation of this front into one grand continuous landing, levee or wharf attracted the early attention of Dr. Lane's comprehensive and scientific mind, and he was prompt in placing it before the public eye for consideration. The St. Louis public then viewed the project as visionary, and the labor as herculean, unnecessary and impossible, and it required years before those interested in its completion could be persuaded to acquiesce in and willingly aid in its execution.

Dr. Lane, however, lived to see his plan universally approved, and so far carried out as to afford berths for more than one hundred steamboats at a time to lie discharging and receiving freight, and crowded by commercial transactions and travelers. This was his chief reward for his services as Mayor, for his yearly salary was but three hundred dollars for performing all the duties of this responsible office.

But few of the benefactors of St. Louis have left a more honorable record of their labors than the first Mayor, and none deserves a more prominent niche in its temple of fame for his example of industry, perseverance and fidelity.

The Marquis de Lafayette had arrived in the United States in 1824 on a national visit, on a formal invitation from all the American people, and was visiting the chief cities in such order as his friends thought most practicable and convenient to himself and son, who accompanied him.

From his first landing at New York the hearts of Missourians were elated with the hope that the great French patriot—the friend of Washington—would gratify them by visiting their State, then the most distant from the centre, and the youngest member of the Federal Union. They, therefore, at a public meeting convened for that purpose, prepared and forwarded by a suitable messenger a most kind and pressing invitation to Gen. Lafayette to visit them at their own distant homes, that they and their children might testify to him in person the love and gratitude they all felt for him for his disinterested devotion to their country's welfare in the day of its greatest need.

To this message the General returned such an answer as might have been expected from one possessing such a well-known benevolent heart, but stated he could not precisely fix on the time when he should have the happiness of visiting his former countrymen, and the land once a part of his own country, but now of his dearest friends.

The answer was entirely satisfactory, and no time was lost in making all the preparation possible to give so distinguished a personage a suitable reception. The whole population seemed to be putting themselves in preparation to participate in the reception from that moment.

He had spent most of the winter of 1824 and 1825 in visiting the people of the Southern States in their chief cities, and had arrived at New Orleans early in April, where communication with St. Louis was more frequent and easy, by which the anxiety of the people to see him was intensified by the glowing accounts given in the journals of the day of his progress, and the ovations tendered him on all sides of his line of travel by all classes of the people.

In short, our language is lean in words to adequately describe the enthusiasm of the people in all sections of the country to do honor to the living friend of Washington, who had come thousands of miles across the great deep at their request to let them look upon the face of the beloved friend of Washington.

In the evening of the 28th of April, 1825, a courier arrived from Carondelet with the news that the Marquis de Lafayette had just arrived there, and would spend the night and come to St. Louis the next morning at 9 o'clock.

The messenger was immediately followed by a dozen other persons hastening to their friends in St. Louis to apprize them of the joyful news, and, as their residences were scattered over the whole city, the information was communicated to every family that night, and every preparation made to witness the imposing ceremony of his public reception.

Many persons from the city spent the night in bringing forward their friends from the country to participate in the general joy and tribute of respect and gratitude.

At length the sleepless night passed away and more of the people of St. Louis witnessed the rising of the sun on that morning than had ever done it on one morning before.

More than half the population of St. Louis, which was then about five thousand, were present about the steamboat landing, the market house and every available standing point, to witness the landing of the most extraordinary, beloved and venerated hero that ever set foot on Missouri soil.

The suspense was short as the boat was prompt to time, coming up close to the Illinois shore and opposite the head of the sand-bar on Duncan's Island, when the prow was slightly turned toward the standing throng on shore.

Here language is wanting to express the sensation of the people as the boat neared the landing and distinct individuals were recognized. No one stood still or kept their muscles still except those of the eyes, which were distended to their utmost capacity and scarcely allowed time to wink.

When the boat began to slacken speed for landing, the group assembled on the boiler deck opened, and Gen. Lafayette, leaning on the arm of his son, walked up to the railing, while a shout such as St. Louis hills never echoed before rose, was repeated and encored until the boat landed, and Gen. Lafayette, assisted by his son, entered a carriage prepared for his reception, followed by the Honorable William Carr Lane, Mayor of the city, Mr. Stephen Hempstead, an officer of the Revolution, and Col. Auguste Chouteau, the chief of the pioneers who laid the foundation of the city.

The carriage was an open barouche, and proceeded up Market street to Main, escorted by Captain Archibald Gamble's troop of horse and by Capt. David B. Hill's company of infantry, thence up Main street to the mansion of Pierre Chouteau, Sen., southwest corner of Locust and Main streets, who had kindly thrown it open for the reception of the General and his friends.

Gen. Lafayette was the guest of the city and was surrounded by its officers who presented and introduced a vast number of citizens to their distinguished guest. Among this number one deserves to be particularly mentioned. This gentleman, then seventy years old, was Alexander Belliseme, who came to America on the same ship with the Marquis on his first visit to America when he came to tender his services to the United States.

The scene was truly affecting when these old French soldiers met after such a long separation and such wonderful vicissitudes as each had passed through. They embraced and kissed each other again and again, and talked over their reminiscences of the trip and its incidents. No one who witnessed it can ever forget it, and there were hundreds present at the time. Just before dinner the General paid a visit on foot to Gen. William Clarke's museum, some hundred yards distant, for his step was yet firm and his eyes still vivid with the animation of youth, being then in the sixty-ninth year of his age. After dinner he visited Missouri Lodge No. 1 of Freemasons, and was received by about sixty brethren and welcomed by the late Archibald Gamble, and both himself and his son, George Washington Lafayette, were elected honorary members of that Lodge, two of whose members then present still survive.

At evening a splendid ball was given at which was the *elite* of the city, and after it a sumptuous supper, in honor of the distinguished guests, and a general illumination of the city.

On the following morning the Marquis with his suit was escorted to the boat by a crowd of citizens, who, as the boat glided down the Father of Waters, cheered him on his way to

Kaskaskia as long as their voices could be heard or their demonstrations noticed.

The progress of Missouri in commercial pursuits had at length attracted the public attention at Washington so far as to induce Congress to survey a mercantile road across the Plains to New Mexico, and an act had been passed for that purpose, and commissioners appointed to superintend the survey and locate the road. As this road is all now out of this State, it may at first view seem to have little to connect it with the history of Missouri, but on a nearer view it will appear that Missouri and Missourians have enjoyed nearly all the advantages of the trade with New Mexico. In June, 1825, Maj. Sibley, who had been appointed one of the commissioners to survey and establish the road, set out with Col. Joseph C. Brown as surveyor, and Capt. Archibald Gamble as secretary, and repaired to Independence, where he fitted out seven wagons laden with goods suitable for trading with the Indians on the route, and Mexicans at the end of the contemplated road, and pushed boldly into the almost interminable prairies of the West, in the direction of Santa Fe, and accomplished the object contemplated in the most satisfactory manner, without loss, delay or the least disappointment to any engaged in it.

This road has been in constant use for more than forty years without visible change in its location, which speaks volumes in praise of the faithful location of it.

Its advantages to Missouri over any other route will prevent any attempt to divert the general direction of the New Mexican trade from this long traveled road.

While these commercial projects were being prosecuted with vigor, objects of a sacred and divine nature received their well-merited attention.

On the 20th of June of this year, Rev. Salmon Giddings consecrated the first Presbyterian church erected in the city. It was located on the northwest corner of Fourth and St. Charles streets.

He had a very respectable congregation,- which he had accommodated with a place of worship for several years, in his private school room, on Market street, opposite the present Court house, where he taught a private school.

The history of St. Louis would be incomplete without the record that Rev. Salmon Giddings was one of its earliest benefactors, was a profound scholar, a faithful teacher and a good man; that many of the most intelligent business men of the State are indebted to him for their scientific, moral and polished education and their success in life.

The demise of Gov. Frederick Bates, on the 1st of August, 1825, rendered an election necessary to fill the executive office, and among the prominent candidates were Col. Rufus Eastou Hon. David Todd, William C. Carr, Esq., and Gen. John Miller. An exciting political campaign followed, resulting from the unsatisfied state of the public mind after the election of John Quincy Adams, in the House of Representatives, by the unexpected vote of Missouri.

The contest resulted in the election of Gen. John Miller for Governor, and Col. B. H. Reeves for Lieut.-Governor.

CHAPTER X.

The Assassination of Mr. Horatio Cozzens—The Seat of Government Removed from St. Charles to Jefferson City—Hon. Thomas H. Benton Re-elected to the Senate of the United States.

Industrial pursuits never had a firmer hold on the people of Missouri than in the spring of 1826. They had seen themselves relieved thereby from the evils of credit and banking systems, and seemed encouraged in their laudable efforts by the ready sale of all their surplus products to the constantly increasing numbers of new comers crowding into the State in search of new homes and a more extended field for their industrial operations and enterprises.

Everything seemed to have a natural growth and stimulant. Trade, though not brisk, was greatly extended and steadily increasing. All freighting was now done by steamboats on all the rivers, and coal began to be used for warming dwelling houses in the city. The mining for lead in the vicinity of

Dubuque, Iowa, and Fevre river and Galena, Illinois, gave great animation to all commercial operations in St. Louis, connected with the trade on the Upper Mississippi, and during the year doubled the trade on that stream, which has increased rapidly since that period. The fur trade on the Missouri was prosecuted with its usual activity, but not in the laborious mode of former years. Steamboats had taken the place of barges; engines had assumed the labors of men, and steam had half annihilated distance and time. Trappers, hunters and voyageurs no longer paid their yearly visits in barges to St. Louis. They were seen no more on the streets, nor heard chatting with their wives and children round the tables spread in the piazzas of their little cottages surrounded with flowers and highly cultivated inclosures. A new age had overtaken and expelled them.

Early in this year the classical department of studies in the St. Louis College on Second street, near the Cathedral, was suspended preparatory to aiding in establishing the St. Louis University on the site it now occupies. It is the first chartered literary institution and deservedly the most celebrated in the city. Its character is as well known and its documents as readily recognized at Copenhagen, St. Petersburg and Moscow as at Rome.

The site of the old St. Louis College is now occupied by immense commercial buildings, and all the professors who ever taught in the institution except one are dead.

Mr. Horatio Cozzens, who examined the senior class of 1829 and eulogized it for its perfection, and who was regarded as the most accomplished scholar in the city at that day, is also dead. His death forms a part of the sad history of St. Louis. Mr. Horatio Cozzens was a lawyer of great eminence and had no equal as an orator or scholar in the city. He was emphatically the French people's shield from the sharpers of that day, as he spoke their language purely and was always accessible to them, being a gentleman of most fascinating manners and kind feelings.

He had just finished the defense of a client before a jury in the office of Justice Penrose, in the old Masonic Hall building, on the north side of Elm street, between Main and Second streets, when French Strother, a young lawyer about twenty-two years old, who was not engaged in the pending suit, but stood near him, intimated to Mr. Cozzens, in low words or by signs, that he wished to have a private interview with him outside the office, and immediately stepped out of the office followed by Mr. Cozzens.

In an instant Mr. Cozzens was heard to say, "You are acting like a savage." Mr. James Sutton, a juror, who was sitting near the window, looked out and saw the two men facing each other, and Mr. Strother with a dirk in his right hand striking over Mr. Cozzens left shoulder into his body, who immediately fell and expired.

Mr. Strother was immediately arrested and committed to jail to await the action of the grand jury. He was confined in a cell with one John Brewer, under sentence of death for perjury in a capital case. On the night preceding the day set for his execution he broke jail, with Strother and several others, most of whom were recaptured; but Strother made his escape to Mexico, where he died a few years since, in the city of Matamoras, in the State of Tamaulipas, of mania potu.

The County Court took action this year for the erection of a court house on the site where it now stands, which it was estimated would cost twenty thousand dollars—considered a liberal expenditure at that time.

As Missouri had but one Congressional representative to elect, a vast field was to be traversed in the canvass, and the candidates commenced their labors early in the spring. Notwithstanding so many of Mr. Scott's former friends had expressed their disapproval of his action in the late Presidential election, he allowed his name to be used in the canvass. He was well known, had many personal friends and the whole strength of the Adams party, and obtained a very respectable vote, of 4,155.

He was opposed by Mr. Edward Bates (brother of the late Governor Frederick Bates), who received 6,635 votes, and was elected.

The victory of Mr. Bates over Mr. Scott did not give the satisfaction to the Jackson party that was generally expected, as he was a very mild, peaceful, philosophic gentleman, who would not transcend a line of conduct that his judgment did not approve to gratify any party or retain office.

His popularity, therefore, was shortlived with those who had elected him, and a successor was sought for before he had entered on the duties of his office.

At this third general election, held on the 7th day of August, 1820, the friends of General Jackson in the Democratic party, as it was afterward called, obtained a very decisive majority, and thus became responsible for all the legislative acts, as a party, for many years thereafter. Its chief distinguishing features were opposition to banks and State indebtedness for internal improvements.

At the session of the Legislature of this year the Chairman of the Committee on Education, Lilburn W. Boggs, recommended memorializing Congress for the selection of the 25,040 acres of land appropriated for seminary purposes.

Then followed a discussion as to the location of the State University, which lasted twelve years, when it was finally located at Columbia, Boone County.

On the 4th of July, 1826, a coincidence transpired that threw the whole American people into mourning, and at once recalled the political events of exactly half a century. Two of the ex-Presidents of the United States expired on the fiftieth anniversary of the nation's birth.

At the commencement of the century they were both competitors for the highest office in the gift of the American people. Mr. John Adams was then the President of the United States; and, on the 4th of March, 1801, retired, and his competitor, Thomas Jefferson, succeeded him, and filled the office satisfactorily eight years, and now they had both expired on the same day, equally covered with glory and honor, and full of years.

They had differed in life only in the means of attaining the same end—the happiness and prosperity of their people.

It became the nation to mourn and to do honor to these departed worthies. They had both assisted to fill the measure of their country's glory, and alike and together had received its homage and approbation.

The sad news had arrived at St. Louis by the slow walk of that day, and on its receipt, Dr. Lane, the Mayor, by a proclamation of 26th of July, convened the people to consider what action it behooved them to take on the mournful occasion, and appointed August the 3d, at 2 o'clock, P. M., in the Baptist Church, for the purpose.

The people assembled pursuant to the proclamation; Judge Peck, of the United States District Court, addressed the audience, with several others, in speeches eulogistic of the departed patriots; after which it was resolved to celebrate the double obsequies on the 7th inst., and due preparations were made for that purpose. The day was devoted to the solemn obsequies. The stores and public places were closed, minute guns fired, flags floated at half mast, and all amusements were suspended in honor of the worthy dead.

The stillness of the following night corresponded with the ceremonies of the preceding day, and afforded a fit season for contemplating other coincidents that attracted the attention of the thoughtful of that day, and are yet worthy of a moment's notice of the lovers of historical facts:

Fisher Ames, the friend and compatriot of those illustrious men, also died on the 4th of July.

John Adams was eight years older than Thomas Jefferson, who was eight years older than James Madison, who was eight years older than James Monroe, who was eight years older than John Quincy Adams, so that each of the four last mentioned persons entered on the duties of the Presidential office in the same year of their age.

The seat of government of the State of Missouri was removed from St. Charles to the city of Jefferson, and the Legislature first met there on the 20th of November, 1826.

At this session of the Legislature, on the 29th of December, Col. Thomas H. Benton was re-elected United States Senator for six years, and was thrice afterward re-elected to the same office, which he filled thirty consecutive years, from the commencement of the State government to the 4th of March, 1851.

CHAPTER XI.

The St. Louis Arsenal Commenced, and a New Market House on Place d'Armes — Missouri Hibernian Relief Society Organized, and a Colonization Society.

The re-election of Hon. Thomas H. Benton to the Senate of the United States showed very distinctly two parties only in the Legislature, and as the representatives had all been very recently elected by the people, the political character of the State was well known early in the year 1827.

The friends of Gen. Jackson soon commenced political organizations under the name of Democrats, when their opponents followed soon after under the name of Whigs, and under these two distinctive names maintained most exciting struggles for a quarter of a century thereafter.

Early in the year Senator Benton, by leave, introduced a bill into Congress to graduate the price of the public lands and to donate to the States in which they lay all that had been offered a certain number of years and all that remained unsold after a certain number of years. This bill he supported with all his ability, assisted by many of the most talented men of the Western States, but failed, as he was opposed by his colleague, Senator Barton, at the most important crisis of his effort, in a most eloquent speech of that distinguished orator and statesman. Strange as it may seem to people of this day, the people of that day believed both their senators acted conscientiously, although so much at variance with each other and yet both as learned. More than forty years have since elapsed, both senators are now dead, the whole subject has been examined and reviewed, and yet the integrity of both remains as brilliant as at that period.

The speeches of both Senators are preserved and the subject is still open. An act of Congress had been passed authorizing the selection of a site for a United States Arsenal near St. Louis, and the present site was selected and building and walling commenced this year, but prosecuted with very little energy that season. The location then was one mile south of the south line of the city which was the mouth of Mill Creek, near the Gas Works. There was then but one bridge across Mill Creek on the south line of the city, and but one road leading southwardly from the city to Carondelet, and not a yard of the distance either paved, macadamized or graded.

A new era, however, was dawning on St. Louis. The old market house on the north end of Place d'Armes, running parallel with Market street (and the only one in the city), was found to be too small for the accommodation of the people dependent on it. The Mayor and Aldermen therefore passed an ordinance for borrowing money for building a market house on the Place d'Armes, parallel with Main street, on the east side of the block, and appropriated it to that purpose, which, by having a town house above and stores below, seemed for a short time to relieve the desideratum.

The erection of this magnificent building, as it then was deemed to be, induced many owners of lots in the immediate vicinity to improve them, and soon gave this part of the city a more animated and commercial appearance, and obliterated most of the old landmarks, except the streets themselves. Improvements seemed not to be confined to this location only; they extended to all parts of the city at the same time.

New brick yards were established, new lumber yards and new quarries were being opened in the suburbs, and sites for new dwellings selected and improved.

The new buildings in progress of construction showed the necessity of having the cross streets graded and some of them paved, and accordingly an ordinance was passed by the city authorities for paving Olive and Chesnut streets from Fourth street to the river, and Green street from Main street to the river.

The confidence which these measures inspired induced the building of a row of two-story dwellings on the north side of Chesnut street, between Main and Second streets, called Kerr's Row, which was the first row of two-story brick dwellings erected within the city on a cross street. The new buildings in progress of erection differed so far in materials and symmetry from what had been in use in former years that all imitation of former style in building was abandoned, and the monuments of French and Spanish architecture rapidly gave place to the new order of improving the city.

The taxes on lots within the city for street improvements were constantly increasing as the work progressed, and stimulated the owners to either build upon them or dispose of them to others who would, and thus vacant and idle lots no longer disfigured paved streets than was unavoidable.

New buildings, new trades, new enterprises in all directions showed themselves, and gave life, vigor and encouragement to every branch of industry.

At this period the French language was spoken in half the families residing in St. Louis, and there was no charitable society of any particular nationality.

Nevertheless it was easier and more speedy for the indigent and needy then to obtain relief among the old French residents and the emigrants of that day than its has ever been since, with all our large systematic and bannered societies of different creeds and nationalities.

The Missouri Hibernian Relief Society was organized this year by the enterprising Irish emigrants, who then outnumbered all other Europeans, except the French. James C. Lynch was the first president, and William Piggott its first secretary.

The object of the society was "to relieve those distressed in their native land and assist those who desired to emigrate to our shores."

There were less than a dozen German families in the city of St. Louis. In the trial of a case of the larceny of a cow, where a German was a material witness, it was with difficulty an interpreter could be procured, until the witness vociferated "David Deshler," who was immediately sent for and brought into court to translate. This incident furnished him with plenty of visitors, as the German immigration to St. Louis was then just commencing, and his urbane disposition attracted all to him who required the assistance of a German interpreter or adviser; and as he would accept nothing for his services, few have been really greater benefactors in St. Louis than David Dreshler, while he resided here.

The colonization of people of color at Liberia, on the coast of Africa, had become a very popular measure in some parts of the American Union, particularly in the slave States, and the friends of slavery, desiring to remove the free colored from the slaves, became, in many instances, its most active advocates and promoters.

Missionary societies also seized on it as a fit channel by which to spread the knowledge of the Gospel among the idolaters of Africa, and gave it their undivided support.

So important a subject could not escape the notice of the enlightened citizens of St. Louis, nor be allowed to pass without action or participation.

A call was, therefore, made for the citizens who were friendly to the measure to meet and consider what action it was proper for its friends in St. Louis and Missouri to take in the premises.

Accordingly, a meeting was held in the Baptist Church, where the St. Clair Hotel now stands, which, for talent, weight of character and unity of sentiment, has never been excelled by a meeting of like numbers in the State, and its selection of officers shows in what light the meeting viewed the subject; and after it had been organized and the object explained and discussed it was determined to form a Colonization Society auxiliary to the American Society, to be called "The St. Louis Auxiliary American Colonization Society," and to elect its officers from the persons present who gave in their names as members.

Twenty officers were then elected from the society in 1828, and now in 1869, after a lapse of forty-one years, they are all numbered with the dead except three. Yet their memories are still brilliant, and form a part of the honorable history of the builders of the fame of St. Louis and Missouri. The following were the officers elected, viz.: Hon. William C. Carr, President; Col. John O'Fallon, Hon. James H. Peck, Dr. Wm. Carr Lane, Hon. Edward Bates, Vice Presidents; Theodore Hunt, Edward Charless, Hon. Henry S. Geyer, Charles S. Hempstead, Thomas Cohen, Hon. Robert Wash, Dr. H. L. Hoffman, Col. Joseph C. Laville, Rev. Salmon Giddings, John H. Gay and Rev. John M. Peck, Managers; Josiah Spalding, Corresponding Secretary; Daniel Hough, Recording Secretary; Henry Von Phul, Treasurer.

The United States had purchased the site on which Jefferson Barracks now stand, and formed a cantonment there, ten miles below the city of St. Louis, and, as in other armies, quarrels occasionally arose among the men and ended in acts of great violence.

Such an occurrence transpired there in this year: one Hugh King, a soldier in the United States Army, murdered a sergeant of his company, and was executed for it after a trial under the laws of the State of Missouri, in the usual form, near the city.

The quadrennial election was to be held in this year, and the most active and efficient preparations were early made by both parties to bring forward all their strength.

There were no railroads or telegraphs in those days, nor many weekly mails; therefore couriers for the distribution of handbills and messages were in great demand and lean horses plentiful.

The country was full of patriots who were willing to serve their country in the offices of that day, although the emoluments were not half equal to those now paid, and thus the State was overrun with patriotic candidates for every office in it. This made lively times for bar-tenders, but sad ones for candidates, cooks and wives who were expected to keep open house during the canvass, although it often emptied both the smoke-houses and the poultry-yards, to their no limited inconvenience.

At length the 4th of August, 1828, arrived, which was to terminate the canvass. Hon. John Miller was the only candidate whose friends continued their candidate's name before the voters for the office of Governor, and was, of course, elected. The office of Lieutenant-Governor was closely contested by five candidates—Samuel Perry, Felix Scott, Alex. Stuart, Daniel Dunklin and Alex. Buckner. Daniel Dunklin was elected. There were three prominent candidates for Representative in Congress at the commencement of the canvass—Hon. Edward Bates, Dr. William Carr Lane and Spencer Pettis, Esq. The first was on the Whig ticket and the two latter on the Democratic ticket, and so nearly did the friends of the last two seem to be balanced that they submitted the question to Col. Benton to say which should be the candidate, to secure the election of one of them. Col. Benton's knowledge of the two candidates enabled him to give a prompt decision in favor of Mr. Pettis, which was promulgated by handbills through the State but a short time before the election.

This decision, which secured the election of Mr. Spencer

Pettis to the United States House of Representatives, also had the effect of keeping the Jackson or Democratic party united for a long time by its example.

A meeting had been held on the 8th of January, 1828, at Jefferson City, by the friends of Gen. Jackson, to nominate an electoral ticket to be voted for at the Presidential election, to be held on the 3d of November of that year, when Missouri had but three electoral votes. Dr. John Bull, of Howard county, Major Benjamin O'Fallon, of St. Louis county, and Ralph Dougherty, of Cape Girardeau county, were nominated electors for the three districts of the State, elected at the Presidential election held on the 3d of November, 1828, and all cast their votes for Andrew Jackson for President and Martin Van Buren for Vice-President of the United States. The friends of Mr. Adams, the President then in office, did not suffer the election to go by default, but, on the 8th of March following, met in Jefferson City and nominated Benjamin A. Reeves, of Howard county, Joseph C. Brown, of St. Louis county, and John Hall, of Cape Girardeau county, as electors, and at the Presidential election in November supported them with the whole strength of the Adams or Whig party, of 3,400 votes—without success, as the Democrats or Jackson party polled 8,272 votes against them, showing 11,672 votes cast at that election in the State.

CHAPTER XII.

The Court House Finished, and an Episcopal Church—The Branch of the Old United States Bank Opened in St. Louis—Inauguration of Water Works System.

The year 1820 opened with flattering indications of prosperity in all parts of the State, and in the city of St. Louis in particular. The Legislature had already formed many new counties, and early in this year altered the lines of some, divided others, formed new ones and defined the county seats, and passed many acts which show that the men of that day saw the signs of the coming greatness of Missouri and prepared to aid it by necessary legislation.

The citizens of St. Louis manifested the same confidence in the growth of the city, and doubled the number of new buildings of any former year. The court house was finished, according to the original plan, which has been altered and greatly enlarged on all sides since, so that few of its original features, except the site, now appear.

The Episcopalians this year erected a neat church edifice, called Christ's Church, on the northwest corner of Third and Chesnut streets, which has long since been removed to give place to the large business houses that now occupy its site; and the same society have since built, and now occupy, that magnificent church edifice at the northeast corner of Locust and Thirteenth streets, and worship in it. This society was formed in November, 1819, and in its progress has done as much to elevate the character of the people of St. Louis as any other by precept and example.

Dr. William Carr Lane, having served as Mayor of the city six years, with credit to himself and satisfaction to the people, declined permitting his name to be used as a candidate for that office, and at the election held on the first Monday in April Daniel D. Page was elected Mayor of the city, and entered upon the discharge of the duties of the office with the entire confidence of the people, which he always retained while he would consent to hold the office. His administration is remarkable chiefly for the inauguration of the present water works system. In the preceding month Gen. Andrew Jackson had been inaugurated President of the United States, and his friends being largely in the majority in Missouri, the hopes of all seemed buoyant and business brisk. The United States Bank was then at the zenith of its financial glory, and its directors observing the flattering condition of the commerce of St. Louis without any banking facilities of its own, established a branch of that institution in the city. The officers appointed over the institution were, at its inauguration, Col. John O'Fallon, President; Henry S. Cox, Cashier; George K. McGunnegle, Clerk, and Thomas U. Duncan, Teller. The Directors, were—William Clarke, Thomas Biddle, Peter Lindell, William H. Ashley, John Mullanphy, George Collier, James Clemens, Jr., Matthew Kerr, Pierre Chouteau, Jr., Edward Tracy, Samuel Perry of Potosi, and Peter Bass of Boone County.

It is very seldom that such a number of reliable business men are thrown together to act on such a wide-spread field, and none probably ever conducted an affair more successfully to its complete termination. The government sustained a loss of only one hundred and twenty-five dollars during the many years the branch operated under the direction of these men.

The introduction of this institution at this crisis was fraught with great advantage to every kind of business, and damage to none, as it had no competitor; and, being guided by persons identified with every local interest, its whole ability was exerted to build up every branch of business and promote the general welfare and improvement of the State and city. Silver coin had then been the circulating medium of the country for many years, and the vast influx of foreigners from many parts of the world had put the coins of nearly all the enlightened nations into circulation among the people of Missouri, so that more than half of the circulating medium was foreign coin, chiefly Mexican dollars, five-franc French or Italian pieces, and Prussian or German thalers. Soon after the opening of the Branch Bank, United States notes and half dollars took the place of all larger coins while the charter of the bank lasted. U. S. Bank notes and half dollars were the chief circulating medium, as Spanish dollars and United States gold were at a premium sufficient to cause their withdrawal from circulation, and very few now exist of older date than 1830.

The improvement of the streets of the city was vigorously prosecuted, according to the original design. Seventh street was widened to sixty feet and extended to the northern line of the city. Fourth street was surveyed to Lombard street, and widened where it was less than eighty feet wide, to that width; and Second street was graded and paved between Olive and Vine streets; and Locust street was also paved from Main street to the western side of Fourth street, and preparations made to gradually extend the pavements through the city. This congeries of facilities for the transaction of business inspired confidence in the certain growth of the city and the increase of its commerce. Several warehouses were erected on the Levee or Front street and several good stores were built on Main street during the year. Some of the early settlers located on Main street had become quite weary of the inconvenience their families suffered by being confined to so limited a space as the expansion of business had forced upon them, and began to build new dwellings in the more retired parts of the city and to allow their old residences to be converted into places of business as the expanding demands required.

The increase in population, as shown by the census, was slow during the decade between 1820 and 1830, in consequence of many old French families who were fond of a rural life retiring into the country, as facilities for their obtaining a subsistence were daily diminished in the city. The hunters, trappers, bargemen and voyageurs also gradually disappeared as new comers of other occupations required their places of residence. Moreover, a very considerable portion of the most industrious part of the population were those who had suffered by the failure of the St. Louis Banks, and, therefore, would not encourage their friends to settle among them until they saw success within their certain grasp thereafter.

The population of the city had only reached 6,004 at the census of 1830, being but little over 2,000 more than it was in 1820. It, however, reached 10,049 in the next decade, being an increase of nearly 10,000.

The year 1830 was rendered remarkable for the general enlightenment of the people of Missouri in regard to the quality of the different kinds of salt they were in the daily use of, and the immense burden that they and all the people of the Western and Southern States had long been subject to, without understanding the disadvantages under which they labored or knowing the weight of the burden they bore.

In the settlement of the Western States the first and great desideratum was a supply of good, wholesome salt, and necessity compelled them at an early day to manufacture it from fountains, more or less impregnated with other deleterious substances, and to use it for a long period before a good article could be procured elsewhere.

At length, with the improvements of the age, the article became plentiful at our great seaports, but covetous rulers had watched its charms, and had seized it as one of the most available objects from which to collect a large revenue, and imposed a tax on it of over two hundred per centum on its cost, and continued it fifteen years, in time of peace, until the people had despaired of relief and nearly forgotten the burden they bore, when they were entirely relieved of it by one of their senators. Missouri now, only in the tenth year of her age, had become celebrated by the wisdom and perseverance of her senators, who were, at that early day, listened to as oracles in the Senate, and one indeed seemed at a later period to have been inspired, and the people had become enlightened as to the weight of the burdens they bore; but as to the qualities and cost of the salt they then used, experiments, science and interest had but partially informed them of the disadvantages under which they were then laboring, and from which there seemed little prospect of relief.

The products of the Western States were then just beginning to make their appearance in the markets of the world, and their qualities were examined and their defects exposed in all their bearings. The immense swine crops of the Western States required such a vast amount of salt for their preservation that its importance as a subject of taxation could not escape the observation of all whose duty it was to frame laws for the people; and that it should have been permitted to burden the pioneers and settlers of the infant States such a length of time under the eyes of such men as then controlled the tariff is one of those inexplicable blunders which posterity may profit by avoiding, but will gain nothing by discussing at this late day or charging upon the selfish actions of those who permitted it.

The speech of Senator Benton on the salt tax, however, forms a part of the history of Missouri (although delivered in the Senate chamber at Washington), as it enlightened the people of Missouri in regard to the quality, value and uses of the different kinds of salt in our markets, and added much to that knowledge which has elevated the character of Missouri meats in all markets where they are exposed for sale.

The District Court of the United States held its sessions in St. Louis in this year, Judge James H. Peck presiding. Among other weighty matters on trial before that court was one in which Auguste Chouteau and others appeared as plaintiffs against the United States, defendant. Col. Luke E. Lawless, a gentleman of profound learning in the law, appeared as chief counselor for the plaintiffs.

In the decision of the suit, which was against the plaintiffs, the Judge delivered a very learned disquisition (which was printed, to the great annoyance of Col. Lawless).

This legal decision was criticised by the senior counsel of the claimants under an anonymous signature in a public paper, for which the publisher was arrested for contempt of judicial dignity, and brought into court, when Col. Lawless declared himself the author, and attempted a justification on the ground that it was only an examination of a judicial decision, and not an attempt to reflect on official dignity.

Judge Peck, however, thought otherwise, and sent him to prison and suspended him from practicing for a time in that court, by way of punishment for contempt. In conformity to that judgment, Col. Lawless went immediately to prison, surrounded by a crowd of his friends. A writ of habeas corpus was soon obtained, and he was released from confinement and repaired to the city of Washington and preferred charges against Judge Peck, before the House of Representives, which impeached him before the Senate.

After a careful investigation the impeachment was dismissed, and Judge Peck continued in office until his death, several years after.

During the progress of these movements in court, prison and Congress society manifested much interest and excitement, as both gentlemen were eminent and acted with dignity; yet in the countenance of each was observable a very unsatisfied mind and disposition that required the exercise of all the philosophy and knowledge of the law they were masters of to keep them in their proper orbits while in the presence of each other. Col. Lawless had his title from the office he had held in the French army under the first Napoleon, and had been admitted to the bar in the Court of King's Bench in his native country, and possessed many other qualifications that would render him distinguished in any situation or society. Few men pass through so many vicissitudes in life as he had by force of circumstances beyond his own control, and yet exhibit no want of energy or ability. Judge Peck was one of the favorites of Minerva, who had from infancy enjoyed her smiles and favors, and in early life obtained the position which, of all others, he seemed best qualified to fill with credit to himself and profit to his countrymen.

Elated by his success and position, he seemed to deem it a duty for him to appear perfect in everything and an example to all, and probably no person in the city at that day displayed a disposition to elevate the character of the people among whom he dwelt more than he in every position where he acted. Col. Lawless was afterward appointed Judge of the Circuit Court of St. Louis county, and filled the office very acceptably many years.

It may appear remarkable that neither of these gentlemen has left a relative among us or a monument of their labors to recall them to memory or enlighten posterity.

CHAPTER XIII.

The Duel between Hon. Spencer Pettis and Major Thomas Biddle, and the Attending Circumstances.

The Twenty-first Congress would complete the term for which Senator David Barton had been elected, and from the well-known state of the political parties no hope of his re-election by the Legislature was entertained by his admiring political friends, who were certain of being deprived of his influence and ability in Congress unless he could be returned to the Lower House at the next election. Early preparations were therefore made, and his name placed prominently before the people as a candidate to represent the State in the House of Representatives, where Missouri had as yet but one member to represent her and many interests that required the attention of an able and experienced statesman.

Under these circumstances Mr. Barton, then a Senator, became a candidate for representative in the Twenty-second Congress, being assured of the support of all the Whig or Adams party, and his personal friends, who were very numerous. The acknowledged ability of Mr. Barton and his long experience in public life made him a formidable competitor in a canvass extending over the whole State of Missouri, against Hon. Spencer Pettis, a very young member of the twenty-first

Congress, about half through his term of office. The canvass commenced with great spirit on both sides, and in its progress led to circumstances which the historian (after a lapse of forty years and the death of all the actors and near relatives who bore their names) can not omit to relate as they transpired without marring the perfection of his narrative of facts as they were made known to the public at the time of their occurrence.

On the part of the Adams or Whig party, as it then and for many years after was known, Hon. David Barton was the only candidate presented, and the whole undivided strength of the party was exerted to secure his election.

The rechartering of the United States Bank was the chief measure he was expected to exert his masterly mind and eloquence on, and as far as he canvassed the State he devoted his attention to the subject.

The Democratic or Jackson party at the opening of the canvass found three persons willing to serve them as representative in Congress—Mr. James Evans, from the southwest part of the State, and Mr. James H. Birch, from the northern part. Each of these gentlemen, after having ascertained the partiality the people felt for the young man they already had in Congress, returned to their homes and supported Mr. Pettis to the end of the canvass.

In the meantime Mr. Pettis returned home and made arrangements for canvassing the State, making appointments through the State where and when he would address the people, and set a time for addressing the people of St. Louis (his place of residence), which he was prevented from accomplishing by indisposition.

In his address to his constituents his remarks were often laden with charges against the conduct of the officers of the United States Bank, of which Nicholas Biddle was President, and an active politician in the Whig ranks.

These speeches of Mr. Pettis were reported in part in the journals of the day, some portions of which reflected on Mr. Nicholas Biddle, who was regarded as a spotless patriot by many at that day, and second to no man out of public office as possessing political power and influence.

His brother, Major Thomas Biddle, was a paymaster in the United States Army, and resided in St. Louis, where he saw the reports of those speeches, and although not a candidate for any office or in any wise connected with the canvass, he attacked Mr. Pettis in a public journal in such a manner that he thought proper to retort through a similar channel and in an equally rude and personal manner.

The severity of Mr. Pettis' strictures threw Major Biddle off his usual course of urbane proceeding, and impelled him to commit an outrage for which he afterward consented to sacrifice his life by way of honorable reparation and atonement.

Mr. Pettis had returned from the interior of the State in feeble health from a bilious attack, about the 25th of July, and took lodgings, as usual, at the City Hotel, his former residence.

Major Biddle was soon informed of his return, and at evening prepared a cowhide and repaired alone to the hotel with his weapon concealed. Early next morning, before any of the lodgers had risen, meeting a black waiter at the door, he asked him to show him to Mr. Pettis' room, which he did. He found the door opening on the piazza ajar, and Mr. Pettis lying in his night clothes on a mattress spread on the floor in front of the door, wrapped only with a sheet, and asleep.

The Major stripped the sheet at once from the person of Mr. Pettis with one hand and applied the cowhide as vigorously as possible with the other, which in a moment brought a crowd on the piazza and put an end to the violence, as Major Biddle hastened out of the hotel without a moment's delay or uttering a word.

This occurrence produced great excitement in the hotel and city at the time, but the feeble health of Mr. Pettis prevented him from making any immediate movement.

Moreover, the canvass went on, and Mr. Pettis was re-elected by a large majority, which showed his party united and largely in the majority in the State. Mr. Pettis waited quietly for the report of the result of the election, which was held on the 2d of August, 1830, and to regain his health to enable him to avenge himself for the injury he had received from Maj. Biddle. Being desirous of placing all the prominent facts in the case before the public in case of any fatal result from a meeting on the street, Mr. Pettis wrote out an affidavit of the prominent facts and went before Justice Peter Ferguson, and, after being sworn to the truth of the statement, was about to take the affidavit to a printing office for publication, when the Justice informed him he considered it his duty to issue a writ on that affidavit and put Major Biddle under a bond to keep the peace, which was immediately done, while Mr. Pettis was present with a few friends.

In the progress of the proceedings it became evident to the magistrate that Mr. Pettis intended to violate the peace, and he put him under a bond also. This induced Maj. Biddle to address a remark to Mr. Pettis equivalent to a promise that if Mr. Pettis would challenge him he would accept it. He was promised that honor by Mr. Pettis, which was fulfilled by a challenge sent the following day, and accepted by him. The next day—Friday, August 27th, at 5 o'clock P. M., on Bloody Island, now East St. Louis—the meeting was to be held for satisfaction, by the parties being duly stationed at the distance of five paces asunder (to be within range of Maj. Biddle's vision, which was very limited), each holding a loaded pistol in his hand. At the appointed time and place every part of the arrangements was punctiliously carried out, and at the first fire, which was simultaneous, both parties fell mortally wounded; and, to conclude the whole affair, they exchanged forgiveness with each other in the arms of death on the field where they had mutually destroyed each other's life.

Mr. Pettis died the next day (Saturday) and was buried on Sunday following. Maj. Biddle survived until Monday following, when he died and was buried on Wednesday with the honors of war by his military associates from Jefferson Barracks. Neither of these gentlemen left children to inherit their names or estates or to be distressed by their reckless folly, but they each left a host of admiring friends, who were pained to see them immolate themselves for such a phantom of glory while such a wide field for usefulness lay spread out before them.

It is pleasant to turn from such tales of strife and blood and relate how the messengers of peace and good will to men were employing themselves at the same time in improving and beautifying the city.

On the first day of August in this year the corner-stone of the cathedral was laid on Walnut street between Second and Third streets with the usual religious ceremonies, and that venerable edifice was completed with all reasonable dispatch, wherein worshiped the whole Catholic population of the city at that time, as they had then no other place of worship. It is the oldest place of worship in the city, as all of a prior date have given place to the commercial pressure which forty years have brought against them, and their sites are occupied by other edifices.

The death of Mr. Spencer Pettis left Missouri without a representative in the lower house of Congress and necessitated another election to fill the vacancy in the twenty-first Congress. A special election was, therefore, ordered by the Governor for that purpose, and the amiable character and known popularity of Gen. William H. Ashley at once pointed him out as the most suitable person to represent the State, now become conspicuous by the actions of her statesmen, and he was elected almost without opposition to that honorable office, which he filled during the remainder of the twenty-first Congress, and the twenty-second also, with that efficiency, silence and success that marked his active and useful life in every position where he was called to act. His thorough knowledge of the vast wilderness of the West, acquired by his own personal travels and observations, qualified him for giving information on all subjects connected with the interests of Missouri and regions in controversy on the Columbia river jointly occupied by the British and the United States for traders and trappers, and caused his society to be sought by the statesmen of that day who valued the Pacific territory, and were striving to rid it of the incubus of a joint British and United States occupancy. His quiet and persistent course in acquainting the State Department with the evils of the joint occupancy and his pressing solicitations for its termination at length had the effect of rousing the people to the danger of a longer continuance of a measure that brought the two greatest maritime nations on the globe to the very verge of war, and by which, even at this late day, it is believed by many that the United States lost territory to avoid war many years after.

The Legislature chosen at the biennial election of 1830 elected Alexander Buckner to the Senate of the United States, to succeed Hon. David Barton, whose term of service would expire on the 4th of March, 1831, after filling the office ten years with most consummate ability and satisfaction to the Federal or Whig partisans, his admirers and faithful supporters for Representative for the twenty-second Congress.

The United States census taken this year showed the State to contain 140,455 inhabitants, of which 569 were free colored, and 25,091 were slaves.

This showed a rapid increase in population, it having been more than doubled in the last decade; and other statistics exhibited an equally flattering condition of everything that tended to the rising greatness of the State.

CHAPTER XIV.

The Erection of the Second Market in St. Louis, on Broadway—The Sympathy of Missourians with the People of Illinois Distressed by the Black Hawk War—Their Response—Excitement in St. Louis by the Veto of the Bank Bill, on July 10th, 1832, by the President—The First Appearance of Cholera.

The most remarkable feature noticed by travelers visiting the West at that time was the activity manifested at St. Louis in transportation by steamboats, as that had become the only mode of conveyance of goods for all the States in the valley of the Mississippi, and the vast territories that received their supplies from this central depot by steamboat conveyance as far as the waters were able to float them.

The appearance of the city, both within and without, had already undergone a remarkable change, and the occupations of many of its inhabitants had, by force of circumstances, been abolished or so altered that it appeared like quite another city in the most populous parts. The lines of Carondelet, or Vide Poche, wood carts were no longer seen or heard entering the city by Second street, or ranged about the thoroughfares waiting for purchasers; nor barges being navigated along the front of the city, nor yawls conveying passengers across the Father of Waters or collecting flood-wood from the river.

A new era had arrived. Science had obtained control of steam and subjected it to the will of men, and compelled it to perform the labors of both men and beasts. Horses on the ferry boats were no longer in use—the "iron horse" had taken their places; and coal as fuel had been substituted for wood to a great extent within the city. The speed of the ferry boats propelled by steam had made yawls unnecessary and useless, and crossing more pleasant and safe.

The view of the city from the opposite shore presented a most animated and variegated appearance. The wharf or front street was in process of formation, improved in some parts and occupied by steamboats in others, while many new stores and warehouses were being erected on the sites of those stupendous ledges that but the year before formed the garden fence (by their perpendicular fronts) of the old possessors' estate.

As yet no steamboat had been built in St. Louis, and the merchants were dependent on the Ohio river steamboats for transportation of the immense quantity of goods distributed by them over the vast space they supplied with nearly every article of merchandise consumed by the inhabitants or used in traffic with them. The movements of the large number of boats owned at so many different points naturally collected a large number of the most enterprising and energetic business men about this central point of receipt and distribution, and made them acquainted with the advantages St. Louis enjoyed over any other place on the Mississippi for mercantile transactions.

To this circumstance may be attributed the establishment of such a large number of enterprising business men in St. Louis from such distant and varied localities about that time, who have since given St. Louis such *eclat* and character abroad for the honor, promptitude and integrity of her merchants and business men that no city on the continent enjoys a fairer fame. This influx of enterprising citizens induced the city authorities to erect the Broadway market to accommodate the citizens of the northern part of the city, which at length attracted more persons about it than could be accommodated, and compelled its removal to give space for the immense mercantile transactions that crowded Broadway. The Missouri

Insurance Company was also incorporated this year, with a capital of $100,000. The interests of St. Louis and Missouri have always been so intimately connected with those of Illinois that any circumstance that disturbs one affects the other, and this was never more clearly evinced than in 1831 during the troubles of the people of Illinois with the Sac and Fox Indians, who had so threatened them that they had suddenly abandoned their homes and fled for safety to places where their families were in danger of suffering for food, which was no sooner known in St. Louis than prompt measures were taken for their relief by a mass meeting of the citizens being called, at which Archibald Gamble, Esq., presided, and George K. McGunnegle acted as secretary.

Hon. Henry S. Geyer addressed the meeting and moved for the appointment of a committee of thirteen to collect subscriptions, which was carried by acclamation, and the names of the committee are a sufficient index of the manner in which their duties were performed. They were—Daniel D. Page, John Kerr, Henry King, Peter Powell, Adam S. Mills, Geo. Sproule, Wm. Finney, Thomas Cohen, John Smith, Joshua B. Brant, A. L. Johnson, J. W. Reed and John H. Gay. This warlike demonstration on the part of the Indians, which agitated the people of Illinois and Missouri more or less during two summers, was incited by a Sac warrior named Macuta Milkacatah (interpreted Black Hawk), born in 1767, and at that time sixty-four years of age, and well known among all Indians as an inveterate enemy to the people of the United States and a friend to the British, from whom he had been receiving presents for the last forty years. He had participated in many battles, and was deservedly distinguished for his merciful and generous character toward the weak and feeble as well as women and children. The removal of all the disposable United States troops from Jefferson Barracks to expel this redoubtable chieftain and his adherents from the lands they had sold in 1804 naturally created the same excitement in Missouri that it did in Illinois, and to some extent suspended emigration to the northern part of the State and greatly reduced the production of lead in the vicinity of Galena, and to that extent, for the time being, seemed to be a disadvantage to St. Louis and all parts of the State. After Black Hawk had violated the treaty made with Gen. Gaines and Gov. Reynolds, the trade of St. Louis seemed not to be affected by the war, as the prompt action of Gen. Atkinson and Gov. Reynolds demonstrated that a period would be put to it as soon as the savage could be overtaken, as they had no means to continue the war, if such folly and murders could bear that name. The total defeat and dispersion of his band at the Bad Axe was undoubtedly the last fighting that will ever be done with Indians on the east of the Mississippi river, as they all have now removed to lands of great longitude on the western side of the river and remote from foreign influence. The army had returned to their quarters at Jefferson Barracks but a very short time, when all thoughts of the campaign were buried in contemplation of the predicted distress and ruin that was to fall on the whole community by reason of President Jackson vetoing, on the 10th of July, 1832, an act of Congress rechartering the United States Bank. An excitement, without violence, followed that has never had a parallel in St. Louis, and produced more animated discussions throughout the State than any subject which has agitated the public mind since the settlement of the country. A meeting of the citizens of the county and city was at once called at the court house to express their disapproval of the action of the President. A large meeting was convened, and among those who participated in the proceedings were some who had been his most sincere friends and supporters for many years. Dr. William Carr Lane was called to preside, and James L. Murray, Esq., acted as secretary. A committee was appointed to draft resolutions expressive of the sense of the meeting on the subject. Messrs. Edward Bates, Pierre Chouteau, Jr., George Collier, Thornton Grimsley, Henry S. Geyer and Nathan Ranney were appointed that committee, who reported resolutions highly commendatory of the action of the bank officers, but censurable of the action of the President. To add weight to the action of the committee and the meeting, Dr. George W. Call and Messrs. Frederick Hyatt, Matthew Kerr, Asa Wilgus, Thomas Cohen and Richard H. McGill expressed their views and experience in financial affairs in formal addresses. These extraordinary proceedings attracted due notice, and soon called forth a counteraction on the part of the President's friends in St. Louis, who assembled soon after in the city hall and called Dr. Samuel Merry to act as President of the meeting, and elected Absalom Link as Vice-President, and appointed Gen. William Milburn to act as Secretary. Col. George F. Strother addressed the meeting in a very lucid, spirited and eloquent manner, and when it was resolved to appoint a committee to draft resolutions expressive of the sense of the meeting in regard to the President's action in relation to the rechartering the United States Bank, Messrs. Edward Dobyns, John Shade, James C. Lynch, Lewellan Brown, B. W. Ayers, John H. Baldwin and Philip Taylor were appointed the committee, who reported a series of resolutions fully sustaining the President's course and action in relation to that institution, which were adopted.

The canvass of the quadrennial election had already been in progress several months. The candidates for Governor were Dr. John Bull, Daniel Dunklin, John Smith and Stephen Dorris, the two former of whom were much the most prominent, and received each a very flattering vote. Dr. Bull received 8,035 votes and Mr. Dunklin 9,121, and was elected—the aggregate vote for Governor being 17,596. Lilburn W. Boggs was elected Lieutenant Governor.

Wm. H. Ashley was elected representative in Congress, over Robert W. Wells, by a majority of 602 votes in an aggregate vote of 18,334 in the State, according to the returns of the thirty-three counties into which the State was then divided.

The United States census of 1830 was unsatisfactory to many persons, as the total number of inhabitants amounted to only 140,452. The census taken by the State authority in 1832, however, satisfied the malcontents that the enumeration must have been correct, as, after a lapse of two years, it had only reached 172,276 in 1832, with only a slight impediment to immigration by the Indian war in Illinois.

Immediately after the war Gen. Atkinson returned to St. Louis and was tendered a public dinner by the citizens, but his public duties compelled him to decline for want of time, which he did in a most thankful and appropriate manner. Soon after the Asiatic cholera made its appearance in several places in the United States and created great alarm. The danger at length roused the people of St. Louis and Missouri, and put them to preparing to meet the affliction with fortitude and becoming Christian resignation. A day of fasting and prayer for exemption from the scourge was appointed, and more piously observed than any day has been since. Yet the dreaded pestilence lingered but little. A portion of the army had been forwarded by the lakes to oppose the Indians, and were attacked by the disease and delayed, while others proceeded to Jefferson Barracks, as the Indian war had terminated, and here the first case on the west side of the Mississippi made its appearance. All communication with the city was for a short time suspended, until September 25th, when two well defined cases occurred in the city, and developed the fact that walls and distance are no certain barriers against cholera. It had invaded the city and many persons were laboring under the premonitory symptoms of the disease, most of whom sank under it soon after.

The sudden deaths of a few struck others with gloom and despair. Added to these, a cool, cloudy state of the weather lent its influence to depress the energy of the laboring classes, and brought them in groups about the street corners to relate the tales of woe they had gathered, which added intensity to the excitement then prevailing.

Under such depressing circumstances all business languished or was suspended, and many persons left the city for a time. It is worthy of remark that those who pursued their usual avocations and made no change in clothing or diet were least affected, and seldom failed of recovery if attacked, while those who fled or stood idle suffered both in body and mind, and more frequently perished.

The pestilence destroyed about four per cent. of the population of the city, numbering 7,000, during the five weeks of its continuance. About the close of autumn Gen. Atkinson returned to Jefferson Barracks, and the prominent citizens of St. Louis renewed their solicitation of his acceptance of a public dinner at their hands, since he had again returned among them.

General Atkinson expressed the most profound consideration of the high compliment paid him by the people of St. Louis, but stated that the late epidemic had destroyed many of his dear comrades in arms, and his sympathy for them and their relatives disqualified him from participating in the offered tribute. He begged to decline the honor, and tendered his most heart-felt thanks for the manifestation of their confidence and kindness.

Hon. Wm. C. Carr at that time occupied the bench of the St. Louis Circuit Court, and had been a resident of the county from near the time of its transfer to the United States. He was well-known as a gentleman of good legal acquirements, and a most useful and exemplary member of society; yet there were many persons in the community who, from political, interested or other motives, desired to have him removed, and for this purpose contrived to have charges and specifications, fourteen in number, preferred against him before the Legislature, where his whole judicial conduct on the bench was carefully examined before both branches of that body.

The examination was lengthy, and related mostly to small things, which showed a very limited state of good feeling between the bench and the bar, amounting nearly to contempt in many instances for each other.

After a full investigation of all the charges and specifications, the Judge was acquitted. He, however, resigned soon after and retired to private life.

CHAPTER XV.

Two Representatives in Congress Elected—The State Enlarged by Act of Congress—How it was Done—Arrival of the Sisters of Charity and Founding of their Hospital—The Legislature Authorizes the Sale of the St. Louis Commons by the City Council, and this enables the Public Schools to commence operations.

The terms of office of President Andrew Jackson and Vice-President John C. Calhoun were drawing near a close, and from many incidents and indications that had come to light in Missouri it was very evident those two names would not appear again together on the Democratic ticket in the State.

The popularity of President Jackson, although somewhat

lessened by his discord with the Vice-President and his opposition to the rechartering of the United States Bank, was sufficiently apparent to insure him the Presidential vote of Missouri for his re-election.

At this crisis Vice-President Calhoun was elected a United States Senator by the Legislature of his own State, in consequence of which he resigned the office of Vice-President and left that to be filled by some other person whose political views comported with the whole party.

The act of Congress making the apportionment of representation according to the census of 1830 was passed May 22d, 1832, which gave the State of Missouri an additional representative in Congress and increased the number of her Presidential votes to four in the electoral college.

Governor John Miller, therefore, in pursuance of an act of the Legislature passed for that purpose, divided the State into four electoral districts and issued his proclamation defining each district, and the Presidential electors were chosen in the districts to which they severally belonged upon very clearly defined party tickets. On the Whig ticket were the names of Henry Clay, of Kentucky, for President, and John Sergeant, of Pennsylvania, for Vice-President. On the Democratic ticket were Andrew Jackson, of Tennessee, for President, and Martin Van Buren, of New York, for Vice-President.

The political views of parties were as well known at that period in Missouri as they ever have been since. One party was in favor of the rechartering of the United States Bank and a protective tariff. The other was opposed to both of these measures, and each voter cast his ballot as if it affected those objects only.

The aggregate Democratic vote was overwhelming in each of the districts, and the four Presidential votes of Missouri were given to Andrew Jackson for President and to Martin Van Buren for Vice-President, who were both elected and entered on the discharge of the duties of their respective offices at the commencement of the twenty-third congressional term, on the 4th of March, 1833.

Missouri was represented in that Congress in the Senate by Thomas H. Benton and Lewis F. Linn, and in the House of Representatives by William H. Ashley and John Bull, all friends of the President and Vice-President and in unison with them on all the leading measures of the administration, one of which was the removal of all the Indians to permanent homes west of the Mississippi river and the white settlements. In this measure Missouri was deeply interested, as that part of the State included in a triangle beyond the old west line of the State and the Missouri river was free Indian territory, very fertile and desirable, but an eyesore and nuisance in possession of savages.

This triangle was desirable for Missouri to possess, and she obtained it in the most honorable and peaceful manner, through the profound statesmanship and wisdom of those four patriots and their personal friends a few years later, aided by their suavity, management and noiseless arguments with their political and personal friends in Congress.

This triangle includes seven of the large, fertile counties of the State which are unsurpassed in point of health, location or beauty, and adds much to the symmetry of the State and its local advantages.

The performance of that important labor has had no parallel in Missouri, or in any of the States of the Federal Union, and can never be overlooked by the critical historian or politician, as it embraced two propositions either generally supposed to be insurmountable and out of reach of the ear of Congress so recently relieved from the thunders of Missouri knocking at its doors for admittance into the Union. One was to enlarge the area of slavery by adding to it free territory, and thus at once alter the Missouri Compromise line, or annul it entirely. The other was to remove Indians from lands they had just received for perpetual homes in exchange for their former possessions and to accommodate them with others in a more distant region, where they would have no river like the Missouri to shield their feeble remnant from the incursions of their more powerful neighbors.

Notwithstanding the unpropitious prospect in view, these indefatigable statesmen applied themselves to the work, and, after a most persistent course of more than three years' duration, finally succeeded in enlarging the largest State in the Union and placing some of the fairest lands of the West in the hands of the most skillful husbandmen with a quietness that elicited the admiration of both the friends and opponents of the measure, and freed Missouri from the incubus of Indian neighbors by the act of the Senate in 1836 confirming the Indian treaty.

While these things were being transacted abroad the progress of events within the State were of the most encouraging and flattering kind. The last annual report of the Wharfmaster, for 1831, showed that sixty different steamboats visited the harbor during the year, making 532 different entries, with an aggregate tonnage of 7,769 tons. The city revenue derived from wharfage on the same amounted to $2,167.

In the spring of 1833 Major Phillips and Dr. William Carr Lane erected the Eagle Powder Mills, which became deservedly celebrated for their production, and continued in operation two years, when they were destroyed by an accidental explosion, and no other has since been erected in the vicinity of the city.

Dr. Samuel Merry was elected Mayor of the city at the April election, but the City Council refused to qualify him, as he held the office of Receiver of Public Moneys of the United States, and was therefore ineligible, and he instituted suit to compel the Council to compliance. The court, however, sustained the Council and adjudged him to pay the costs. An election for Mayor was then ordered, at which John W. Johnson was elected, and, being re-elected in 1834, continued in office until April, 1835.

The cholera re-appeared in 1833, in milder form than in the preceding year, but as it continued several months longer, it was as detrimental on the whole to the mercantile interests as in the former year. It seemed, also, to check immigration and enterprise, and cast a kind of gloom over melancholy minds and rendered their energies feeble and inert.

On the 22d of September of this year, 1833, the Secretary of the Treasury, in accordance with the directions of the President, removed the deposits of the United States from the United States Bank to certain State Banks, and was sustained in it by the members of Congress from Missouri and a large majority of their constituents, whose views on this subject were known to accord with theirs.

The society of the Sisters of Charity, which was founded in Paris, in 1046, by St. Vincent of Paul, had extended its reputation for pious acts of mercy throughout the different kingdoms of Europe and into more distant parts of the world. At length, in 1832, their fame had reached St. Louis and enlisted that well known philanthropist, the late John Mullanphy, among their most powerful supporters and contributors, who, aided by the Catholic Bishop of St. Louis Diocese, invited a colony of them to locate a hospital in the city of St. Louis, and offered them a site for that purpose on the south side of Spruce street, between Third and Fourth streets. They accepted it soon after and put it in operation, with limited numbers for want of room, but to the great relief of many afflicted invalids. To aid them in the erection of suitable buildings for the accommodation of their numerous patients the Legislature of Missouri authorized a lottery, by which the sum of ten thousand dollars was raised, which was most economically expended in erecting portions of those substantial buildings known as the Sisters' Hospital, to which they have added many others.

This institution has been in constant action every day since it opened, with the quietude, regularity and beneficence of the sun, and has now attained such a fixedness in the minds of St. Louisans that they would as soon entertain the thought of being bereft of the one as the other.

The history of their merciful doings in St. Louis would fill a volume; and that all their labors and watchings were bestowed upon strangers and no record kept of the names of those that performed them, or any reward hoped for or expected in this world, makes the institution revered by the good and avoided by the bad as holy ground.

Strange as it may appear to people of this day, there had been no scales for weighing hay, coal or cattle in St. Louis until the spring of 1833, when the City Council established one near the southeast corner of the market, on Front street. At this one point all heavy weighing was done for several years after it was established, and no where else in the city. Coal was sold by the bushel before that time, measured in wagon-beds by a qualified person, who generally gave as good satisfaction as our weighers do at this day. Hay was sold by the load, as the parties interested agreed.

The public lands near the city had nearly all been sold, and the amount of cash withdrawn from circulation through the land office was small; but the immense immigration to the State caused large sums to be put in circulation in payment to individuals for new homes, and thus great animation was visible in all departments of business and money plentiful.

The growth of the city was steady and rapid, and the current of business swelling with astonishing acquisitions. This prosperity is evinced by the Wharfmaster's report of 1835 being more than double that of 1831. The number of boats was, in 1835, exclusive of barges, 121; aggregate tonnage, 15,470 tons; 803 entries, and $4,573 wharfage collected.

Over all this rising greatness hung a dark curtain. St. Louis had no Public Schools. The streets swarmed with idle children and public school lands laid unoccupied in the most populous parts of the city; but a luminous day was near at hand that has quite dispelled the gloomy prospect. In March of this year the Legislature authorized the people of St. Louis—as it was bounded in 1812—who owned lots to authorize the City Council to sell the town Commons, a tract of about two thousand acres of most beautiful grounds, and to appropriate nine-tenths to the improvement of the streets of the city and one-tenth to the support of Public Schools. This trifling sum, however, raised the curtain and laid the foundation for the first Public Schools of St. Louis, by which the whole population of the city was enlightened in regard to the advantages of a well regulated Public School system and induced to vote a tax on themselves to establish the present Public Schools.

It may be viewed as a digression from the general history to pursue this subject here, but when the whole State is seen adopting, or rather practicing, as far as possible, the same system, no more suitable occasion than the present may occur to narrate its first movements and entire success in the city. Two small two-story brick houses were erected from the proceeds of the Commons' sale and a small amount collected from rents of lots, and a male and female school opened in each of them in 1837. It was soon found that those establishments, although large enough for ordinary common country schools, were quite inadequate for the accommodation of the number of pupils in a city like St. Louis, and the Legislature was applied to for aid. An act was thereupon passed tantamount to an act to tax themselves if a majority voted in favor of it. This was effected, and from that time the Board of Directors of the St. Louis Public Schools (who serve without pay) have brought the schools to the high position they occupy to-day—the pride of the city, its monument of wisdom, its example for posterity, its unspeakable boon to the living.

CHAPTER XVI.

Rise and Progress of Parochial and other Schools and Colleges.

The Public Schools are not the only places that the people of St. Louis can point to with pride as seats of learning, where all the sciences are taught with as much accuracy and perfection as those instituted, endowed or supported by the laws of the State. Many of the most magnificent buildings of the city are seats of learning—used only for that purpose—to which the State has never contributed one dollar, and yet they are filled to overflowing with pupils who will compare favorably with those of our best public schools or colleges.

The most generally attended are the Catholic Parochial schools, male and female; the schools of the Christian Brothers, the schools of the Sisters of Charity or Orphans' Schools, the Academies of the Visitation and of the Sacred Heart, and the St. Louis University. In most of these institutions the patrons pay a fair fee if they are able; if not able to pay, the pupils are taught gratuitously, and there are many in this condition. To these should be added the Washington University and the Mary Female Institute, both under the patronage and tuition of Protestants of the first class of scholarship, well patronized and enjoying wide-spread fame. Thus the people of St. Louis have provided themselves with facilities for educating the rising generation equal to those of any city on the American continent, and have the most flattering prospects for further progress before them. None of these schools have required any religious qualifications of students, but a respectful conformity to rules of order during the time devoted to religious exercises is required in all of them. Two medical schools or colleges have been established in St. Louis, chiefly by private munificence and enterprise, in which many young gentlemen have been educated who now adorn their profession in the vast regions of the West, and have given McDowell's and Pope's Colleges deserved celebrity in the medical world, and placed the names of their founders high in the temple of fame as benefactors to mankind and profound masters of surgery and physic.

The Legislature, at the request of the founders, has given these two seats of learning other names and regulations, but the public has become so long accustomed to calling the institutions after the names of their founders that any other names would be unrecognized by St. Louisans if used in the city. The history of St. Louis can not be written without the name of Joseph N. McDowell being mentioned among its most enlightened and generous benefactors, for the pains he had taken to amuse, instruct and gratify them. He had collected a very valuable and rare museum some time previous to his death and donated it to the city of St. Louis, which was destroyed during the late civil war in the room the city used for its preservation.

These institutions have risen in such quietude and progressed with such stillness and regularity that it is difficult to determine precisely at what time many of them went into use and operation. They seem to have risen up when they could no longer be dispensed with, and are kept in operation by the force of necessity and practical usefulness. The commercial class of colleges, with pupils of riper years and without the stately edifices that attract the gaze of the wondering crowd, has had great influence and much success in forming the character of the business men of St. Louis and others spread over the Southern States and Territories.

They, like the medical colleges, have had a little of the legislative breeze passed gently over some of them, but all the nourishment and gilding they have enjoyed has been derived from the indefatigable exertions of the able professors who conducted them and their patrons.

Private enterprise has kept open many schools in different parts of the city, in different languages and in different sciences, so that no one has thirsted for knowledge who has had the means of making a reasonable remuneration. Thus, painting, drawing, dancing, vocal and instrumental music, telegraphing, photographing and other useful arts have had as skillful professors as were to be found in any of our American cities, and have been as well patronized, so that Missourians, when abroad on the Eastern continent, have found no difficulty in being acknowledged by the most learned men of the world as their equals, and obtaining from them all the knowledge they are able to impart, either of their own country or the distant regions beyond those they may have visited. These improvements, accumulations and acquisitions have all been made in this century, and mostly within forty years. There is not one stone lying upon another in the way of improvement that has not been placed there within the recollection of some of the persons who pass it daily.

CHAPTER XVII.

Destruction of the Old Cathedral by Fire—The First Railroad Convention in St. Louis—The Murder of Deputy-Sheriff Hammond and Burning of the Murderer by the Citizens—The Texan War, in which some Missourians Participated.

The year 1835 opened with cheering prospects for the growth and prosperity of St. Louis. The sale of the Commons it was fondly hoped would produce a sum sufficient to improve some of the principal streets leading into the heart of the city and aid the Public Schools to commence operations.

The Central Fire Company was organized and equipped with a good engine—with human *power;* the only *one* in use at that day for extinguishing fires—and was soon called forth to test its utmost capacity on two of the largest buildings of the city.

The first was the old, unfinished, brick Cathedral, one hundred and thirty-five feet in depth and forty feet in front, with walls twenty-five feet in height, used as a wholesale crockery warehouse by the late Ringrose D. Watson, who had a very extensive stock of goods in it—fortunately well insured.

The second was a livery stable, about fifty feet front by one hundred feet in depth, built entirely of wood, well filled with hay and grain, and having about one hundred horses in it, with carriages and furniture, owned by the late John Calvert, and standing about twenty feet westward from the old Cathedral, on Market street, where Concert Hall now stands.

Both these buildings were destroyed in the heart of the city, with about fifty horses and much other valuable property; but the lesson it taught the citizens, who were nearly all present at the fire, has probably been more beneficial to the growth of the city than that property ever could have been if allowed to occupy that valuable central locality.

This great conflagration, for such it was then considered, commenced in the stable about eleven o'clock on the night of the first Monday in April, 1835, just as the counting of the votes closed in the three wards of the city that showed the election of Hon. John F. Darby as Mayor of the city of St. Louis.

A young, efficient, enterprising and energetic man then took the reins of the city government—one who had become identified with the interests of the city, knew its wants and was willing to devote himself to the promotion of its rising greatness, and who was re-elected the three following years.

Several great interests then engaged the attention of the people of St. Louis and incited them to action. The first was the Great National Road being built across the Union, which would pass through the great western cities; and as its location had arrived at a point where a divergence from a line leading directly to St. Louis might greatly affect its interests, the young Mayor lost no time in delay, but promptly convened the people by proclamation to memorialize Congress to construct the road through St. Louis in its extension to Jefferson City and regions further west.

The meeting convened according to proclamation, at which the Mayor presided and Geo. K. McGunnegle acted as Secretary, when a memorial was numerously signed and forwarded to Congress.

There had been great excitement in some of the neighboring cities in consequence of the lawless conduct of gamblers, loafers and vagabonds; and to prevent their making a similar commotion in this city by congregating or locating in the vicinity, early action was taken by the Mayor's court to rid the city of idlers and corrupters of the public morals, and thus avoid the high-handed measures which had been adopted in some of the neighboring cities to relieve themselves from the baneful presence of such unworthy people.

The punishment of a few of the most prominent among them, by the sentence of the Mayor to imprisonment, so intimidated the fraternity that they gave him a wide field to exercise his authority over, so that, by the assistance of the city marshal and his deputy, the city enjoyed good order during his administration, at small cost.

The utility of Railroads had so far developed itself that the enterprising citizens of Missouri determined in the early part of the year to call a convention to consider what it behooved Missouri to do with the new and wonder working system of conveyance, and, accordingly, a convention met on the 20th of April, 1835, at the court house in St. Louis, composed of sixty-four members from eleven of the most populous counties of the State.

The Convention was organized by calling Dr. Samuel Merry to the chair and appointing George K. McGunnegle Secretary, for organization, when Harry Smith was elected President, James H. Riff Vice-president, and G. H. McGunnegle Secretary. After discussing the subject that had brought such a large number of the prominent citizens of the State together, they examined the feasibility of applying the new system beneficially to transportation on two routes, one to Bellevue Valley, via Iron Mountain and Pilot Knob; the other to Fayette, in Howard county.

Great unanimity and kind feeling prevailed among the delegates during the session, and the St. Louis delegation put a seal on the whole proceedings by giving a festive dinner to the members of the Convention at the National Hotel, now St. Clair Hotel, at the corner of Market and Third streets, which added zest and eclat to the harmonious proceedings of the Convention.

This social entertainment was presided over by Hon. John F. Darby, Mayor of the city, assisted by seven Vice-presidents, viz.: Hon. Hugh O'Neil, Gen. John Ruland, Thomas Cohen,

Esq., Gen. William Milburn, Beverly Allen, Esq., Col. J. W. Johnson and William G. Pettis, Esq. Col. Charles Keemle acted as Secretary.

These eight last named gentlemen are all removed "to the great city of the dead," but the hopes they entertained have been already realized and more extended projects executed—based on their initiatory labors—than their minds had been led to contemplate in all their kaleidoscopic anticipations at that day.

The County Court, considering the importance of the movement, appropriated two thousand dollars to defray the expenses of the Convention, and the whole community manifested the deep interest they felt in this novel improvement by availing themselves of every opportunity to acquire information in relation to it.

At this period the Mississippi river passed the city in two streams of about equal size, being divided by Bloody Island, now part of East St. Louis.

This was an alarming circumstance to owners of real estate in St. Louis, as the current on the eastern side of the island was daily increasing, while that on the western side was daily decreasing, and threatening to leave no channel on the west side of the island.

For a city of 15,000 inhabitants, like St. Louis, to be forsaken by a river like the Mississippi, may be a grand subject to contemplate, but a sad misfortune for the inhabitants to suffer. Yet this was allowed to continue a quarter of a century without an effort being made to prevent it.

The departure of so large a portion of the river from its western shore slackened the velocity of the current and allowed the muddy water from the Missouri to deposit the heavy sand it held in suspension near the shore in front of the lower part of the town, where the stream in 1800 was seventy feet deep, until it formed a sandbar on which vast quantities of flood-wood lodged and defended the accumulations until assisted by a growth of willows, cottonwood and sycamores it had become in one lifetime an apparently permanent island and one of the most unsightly spectacles ever exhibited to the people of St. Louis. It was then known as Duncan's Island,

and so named from the first occupant who cultivated a small portion of it as a cornfield in 1835.

Its presence in the former deep channel of the river quite ruined the navigation along its bank as far as it extended, and its rapid growth up stream gave signs that it would eventually thrust itself like a wedge between Bloody Island and the city, and thus destroy the port entirely.

It had progressed so far northward that no steamboat could land below Market street, and some boats had grounded directly in front of and east of the Merchants' Exchange before those most interested could be brought to contemplate or see their danger and damage. However, when those most interested were roused to a sense of their situation, they instructed their representatives in Congress to aid in obtaining govermental assistance in its removal. The sum of fifteen thousand dollars was first appropriated for a preliminary survey and examination of the river and harbor, and Major R. Lee, of the U. S. Engineer Corps, sent to survey and superintend the work. Subsequently the further sum of one hundred thousand dollars more was appropriated to finish the work. The latter sum was never expended as contemplated by Major Lee's system of improvement, as the proprietors of a tract of land laid out into town lots on the Illinois shore obtained an injunction against Major Lee and prevented the completion of the work, which resulted in a change of the system of improvement more satisfactory now to all parties than that formed by Major Lee, but not executed until many years later. By the latter system Bloody Island has become a part of the flourishing city of East St. Louis. The Father of Waters now passes between the two cities in one undivided stream as it did one hundred years ago, and the sand-bar, or Duncan's Island, has been washed away or forms a part of the city landing.

A quadrennial election was to be held in August of this year, 1836, at which a Governor and Lieutenant-Governor were to be elected, and, as was customary with Democrats in the days of General Jackson's administration, the leaders of the party met on the 8th day of January, at Jefferson City, and nominated candidates for the first offices of the State. Lilburn W. Boggs was nominated for Governor and Franklin Cannon for Lieutenant-Governor of Missouri.

At a later period the Whig party nominated William H. Ashley for Governor and James Jones for Lieutenant-Governor. All these four candidates were gentlemen of acknowledged ability and of spotless fame, and, as far as they were concerned, the whole canvass was conducted in the kindest and most quiet manner, and the result acquiesced in without the least apparent dissatisfaction by the vanquished party. For Governor Lilburn W. Boggs received 14,815 votes, and was elected. Gen. Wm. H. Ashley received 13,057 votes for the same office, which showed that 27,872 voters visited the polls at this election. Franklin Cannon received 13,402 votes for Lieutenant-Governor, and was elected. James Jones received 10,210 votes for that office, and 53 votes were cast for other candidates for the same office.

In the summer of this year there arose in St. Louis one of the most sudden, violent and tragic excitements that a historian has occasion to record, which, from its intensity, produced results that horrified the quiet, Christian community in which they transpired, and caused the day on which they occurred to be made an epoch for a quarter of a century following.

Mr. William Mull, a deputy constable, had arrested one of the hands of a Pittsburg steamboat and was escorting him to a Justice's office when they met another hand from the same steamboat, named McIntosh, a negro, who asked the prisoner where he was going, and on being answered, McIntosh said to the prisoner, "run away," which the prisoner (who was without a coat) attempted to do, but was at once caught by the shirt-sleeve and held by Mull, with his arm and hand partly out of it. The prisoner told McIntosh to cut off the sleeve, which McIntosh did, and the prisoner escaped. Mull dropped the sleeve and arrested the negro, who made no resistance, as a crowd had gathered, some of whom accompanied Mull and the negro to the Justice's office. The Justice examined the case and required bail, which the prisoner was unable to obtain, and was, therefore, ordered to jail on a mittimus delivered to the deputy, Mull, who, having no fear of personal danger, took no notice of the knife the negro had cut the shirt-sleeve with, and walked with his prisoner down Third street from Olive to Chesnut, thence up Chesnut to Fourth street, where the crowd that followed them thus far dispersed, and Mull, having crossed Fourth street to the Court-house block, which was then surrounded with a brick wall, met the Sheriff's deputy, Mr. Geo. Hammond, who seeing Mull, a middle-sized man, about forty years of age, left alone to conduct a large, powerful negro of twenty-six years to jail, kindly offered to assist him in escorting his charge to the jail, still two blocks distant. Mull accepted his assistance, and all three were walking on the sidewalk near the northeast corner of the Court-house block, with Mull on the right, the negro on his left, between him and the wall, and Mr. Hammond a yard or two in the rear.

Francis L. McIntosh, the negro, who had been sullen and silent until then, said (turning partly back and addressing Mr. Hammond): "What can they do to me for cutting off the shirt-sleeve?" "I don't know," replied Mr. Hammond, and in jest added: "Perhaps hang you." In an instant the negro jerked his right arm from the left arm of Mull, and seizing his boatman's knife aimed a thrust at Mull's throat, which missed, and was repeated, inflicting a terrible wound in Mull's left side. In the commencement of the attack on Mr. Mull the Deputy Sheriff, Mr. Hammond, seized the negro by the collar and pulled him a little back, when he suddenly faced Mr. Hammond and, being held by him, aimed a blow at that officer's throat, entirely severing the arteries of the neck. His blood spurted on the Court-house yard wall in a frightful stream as Mr. Hammond ran round the northeast corner of the square toward his own home, until he fell from loss of blood and expired where he fell before the least assistance could be given him.

The assassin fled, with Mull sadly wounded and in pursuit, shouting, "Catch him! Catch him! Catch him!" until he fell from loss of blood. The citizens in the streets took up the cry and continued the pursuit with great energy and success, as some of those who had heard of the first offense at the Justice's office were yet on the street and joined in the pursuit and in the hue and cry. The negro, outrun by swift-footed lads and headed on the streets by many men, attempted concealment in a garden, and was finally captured there, from whence he was taken and committed to jail by the properly authorized officers of the law.

In the meantime the sad news reached the wife of the murdered officer, who ran with her four children to the murdered father and husband lying in his blood on the pavement, filling the air with their cries and lamentations.

The news spread widely and swiftly, as the sun was setting and the crowd increasing. One officer was murdered, and another said to be mortally wounded in the discharge of his duty, and his wife and children in nearly the same distress as the other.

Reason gave place to rage and sympathy to vengeance in view of the atrocity of the crime and wide spread distress his wickedness had occasioned without the least possible provocation.

The crowd, constantly increasing, seemed incited by the Furies and cried "Hang him! hang him!" and began to move with shouts toward the jail, when the sentence was changed to "Burn him! burn him!" and it moved with increased speed and size to the jail when their phrenzy and terrific demonstrations so alarmed the jailor that he complied with the threatening demands of a countless multitude and gave up the key of the cell in which McIntosh was confined, when he was speedily reached and dragged, trembling, to the street amid the yells of the exasperated crowd, calling for vengeance on the murderer of one of its most prominent and beloved citizens.

There was no delay but to clear a passage through the crowd for those who could reach him, to push, pull and rush him into Chesnut street, and along that street to a point near the corner of Chesnut and Seventh streets, a few yards north of the present site of the Polytechnic building, where stood a small locust tree, to which he was bound with chains preparatory to burning him in the most summary manner.

The wretched culprit, now convinced that he was in the hands of both his judges and executioners, who would inflict certain death on him, begged to be hung or shot at once, as he saw the brush, bark and dry wood from Bobb and Letcher's brickyard being placed around him for his destruction.

Thus far no opposition had been offered to the overwhelming tempest of vengeance without law, but, for the credit of St. Louis and the perfection of its history, it should be stated that most strenuous opposition, expostulation and entreaties were then made to this highhanded, uncommon, illegal and cruel proceeding by one person, who, if he had done no other good act in his life to entitle him to immortality on the page of history, this action at this crisis should do it.

Mr. Joseph Charless, a young man, son of the founder of the *Missouri Republican*, had returned to his home at the southeast corner of Market and Fifth streets, after McIntosh had been committed to jail, when he learned that a crowd had come from the jail into the street and were going westwardly. He immediately followed and arrived with it at the fatal locust tree, and witnessed the hasty preparations for the execution.

This he determined to oppose, and being a good scholar and a pleasant speaker, commenced a harangue to dissuade the crowd from this lawless proceeding and to return the murderer to the jail to await the due process of law.

As no attention seemed to be paid to his address he feared he had not been heard, as he was of moderate size, and asked one of his friends to hold him up in his arms until he could make himself better heard and understood by the people.

His friend grasped him below the knees and held him up above the crowd while he made one of the most earnest, sensible and humane appeals to the wise and peaceful judgment of the crowd that has ever been delivered to maintain and enforce the laws and to dissuade them from their cruel purpose.

In the meantime the impetuous crowd fired the fatal pile and stood silent and aghast, while the most piercing cries, shrieks and moans of the suffering victim rent the air and filled the minds of the beholders with indescribable horror and aversion as the miserable victim, writhing in varying contortions, expiated his terrible crime and ended his mortal sufferings in the flames.

This unlawful proceeding was not popular on the whole, although so far tolerated by the criminal courts that no one was prosecuted, being shielded by the old doctrine of "Vox populi vox Dei."

The day of these sad transactions became a kind of epoch for the following quarter of a century.

St. Louis, estimated to contain 15,000 inhabitants in 1836, had neither public school, bank, park, theatre or library of its own creation for their use, enjoyment or amusement.

Yet taste, energy and enterprise were not wanting to acquire all these things, and through the exertions of Messrs. N. M. Ludlow, F. H. Bebee, H. S. Cox, L. M. Clarke, C. Keemle and J. C. Laveille, a lot was purchased on the south-east corner of Third and Olive streets, where the Postoffice now stands, sixty feet in front and one hundred and sixty feet in depth, upon which a well constructed theatre was erected and operated for many seasons, until several of the proprietors had either died or removed, and the United States purchased it and built the present custom house, subtreasury and postoffice on its site.

The Central Fire Company also purchased a lot and became incorporated. They built a fine brick engine house and a splendid hall (in those plain days) over it, which they used for nearly thirty years, until steam engines and paid firemen superseded them, to their great delight and satisfaction.

Some of the best men St. Louis was ever proud of have been members of the company, and will be remembered through this century for their noble deeds and daring at the mighty conflagrations which they combated during its active career.

The State of Texas had revolted from the Mexican Republic and was the theatre of a sanguinary war, and about one hundred enterprising young men from Missouri had gone in the preceding year to assist the Texans, who were, many of them, their friends and relatives from Missouri and other States.

This circumstance enlisted the sympathy of Missourians in the Texan cause almost as much as the Texans themselves. About forty had gone from St. Louis; Mr. Austin among the number, after whom the town of Austin was named.

The slaughter of the Texans at Goliad, with many smaller parties, and the butchery of women and children by the Mexicans, had quite exasperated the Missourians against them, and caused them to desire their destruction.

The news of the retreat of Gen. Houston in rear of all the women and children of Western Texas, for their protection, to the swollen stream of San Jacinto, followed by a Mexican army threefold more numerous than his own, for their destruction, had so excited the news-reading people of St. Louis that they awaited the arrival of each steamboat from New Orleans with breathless anxiety for many days to learn the sad fate of Sam Houston and the Texan women and children exiled from their homes by the Mexicans.

Words can not describe the joy depicted in every countenance soon after, from overflowing grateful hearts, when a steamboat at length arrived with a passenger from San Jacinto standing on the boiler deck as the boat touched the landing, yelled out to the crowd on shore, "Sam Houston has whipped Santa Anna and got him a prisoner." The mixed crowd tried to cheer, but joy and anxiety to hear more and the rush on board prevented a united huzza which every one seemed to make involuntarily as they rushed on the boat to learn that Texas was free, the war ended, both armies gone home, and the Mexican President a prisoner, coming through the United States.

No news was ever more joyfully received in Missouri than the victory of San Jacinto. It was without alloy, as no Missourian had lost his life there. Missourians then felt as though they had given life to Texas through Aus'in, and that Tennessee had given it liberty through Crocket and Houston.

Thus it happened that the most common watchwords among Missouri's soldiers in the war with Mexico, ten years later, were *David Crocket, Sam Houston, Austin, San Jacinto*, or *Lone Star*, and time has not entirely obliterated their memory yet in Missouri.

Among the polished gentlemen who have graced the social circles of St. Louis and Missouri, and left a lasting impress of his urbanity, dignity, learning and other virtues, no one has distinguished himself more than Hon. James H. Peck, Judge of the United States District Court of Missouri, over which he presided sixteen of the first years after Missouri formed her Constitution, and died on the 1st day of May, 1836.

He was a gentleman of very fine scholastic attainments, and one of those desirous to communicate his knowledge to others. He assisted to form the literary Association known as the St. Louis Lyceum, in 1831, composed of such members as Hon. J. B. C. Lucas, Hon. Henry S. Geyer, Rev. Thomas Horrel, Rev. Mr. Davis, Hon. Wilson Primm, Beverly Allen, Dr. Wm. Carr Lane, Hon. John F. Darby, John C. Dennis, Hon. Peter Ferguson, and others, which continued to flourish until his death, since which it has not convened, although its records are yet preserved by the Historical Society of St. Louis.

CHAPTER XVIII.

The Appointment of Hon. Robert W. Wells to the Bench of the United States District Court of Missouri—The Burning of the First Steam Flouring Mill in the City—Incorporation of the Bank of the State of Missouri—Overthrow of Rev. Elijah P. Lovejoy's Printing Press by a few Individuals under Cover of Darkness of Night—Organization of Gen. Richard Gentry's Command, their Distant Campaign in Florida, and his Honorable Death in the Arms of Victory.

On the 1st of July the appointment of Hon. Robert W. Wells, by President Andrew Jackson to the bench of the United States District Court of the State of Missouri (made vacant by the death of the late Hon. James H. Peck) was made public in St. Louis, and he entered on the discharge of the duties of the office.

No surprise or laudation at the appointment was expressed by the people, as he was a gentleman of spotless fame and fine abilities, and had devoted himself to the study of the laws of his country rather than the schemes of political aspirants, and could enter on the discharge of the duties of the office without further preparation or embarrassment.

The most sanguine expectations of his friends were gratified by his successful course of conduct in office, as he applied himself to his own duties and took no part in the exciting elections of that year or thereafter.

The growth of St. Louis seemed to be accelerated this season by the subdivision and sales of the Common tracts and of the lands divided among the heirs of the late Col. Auguste Chouteau, which allowed the city to expand in a southern direction.

The enterprise of many persons was also directed to the northern part of the city, where great facilities for manufacturing lumber existed, and many persons had made very extensive essays at it and other branches of manufacturing with great success.

In short, the people in the northern part of the city began to show that they intended to make that an important part of a manufacturing city.

Among those who are deserving of mention for their enterprise at that time there were none more conspicuous than Capt. Martin Thomas, who erected a large stone steam-mill for manufacturing flour, lumber and lead, which excited the ambition of his neighbors to undertake other enterprises in the vicinity, which resulted in rapidly advancing the improvement of that part of the city.

Unfortunately for Captain Thomas and that part of the city, after he had it in full operation, on the night of the 10th of July, 1830, the whole establishment took fire and was consumed, with all its contents, without a single dollar of insurance upon any part of it or the contents.

The days of evil tidings in the midst of an electioneering canvass were present. A bill had passed the United States House of Representatives to build the National Road through St. Louis to Jefferson City, and was amended in the Senate, passed and sent back to the House of Representatives for concurrence on the 3d of July, the day of the appointed adjournment, when, for want of time, it was not acted on, and has not been spoken of since in Congress.

The same mail that brought this unpleasant news also brought the sad news of the death of ex-President James Madison, who died at his country seat in Orange county, Virginia.

During the political canvass of that year the two parties were so nearly equal that they watched every circumstance that seemed to affect either party. In their scrutiny, religious papers were examined as well as others.

There was published at that time in St. Louis a gazette by the title of *The St. Louis Observer*, edited by Elijah P. Lovejoy, in which several articles had appeared calculated to offend a certain class of persons and yet not make the editor amenable to the law or responsible to a particular individual.

Late in the night of the 21st of July a party of those persons who kept late hours about ale-houses, beer-shops and saloons, and possessed but a moderate stock of cash, character or interest in the reputation of the city, broke open the publishing room of the *Observer*, overthrew the presses, threw and scattered the types into the street, and separated instanter without further violence. The city officers made one or two arrests, and one person was tried the next day, who was found not guilty and discharged. The result, however, of this trial convinced the editor that the people of St. Louis would not tolerate such publications, and having collected the scattered types, he withdrew from the city only to meet a more fatal opposition.

The progress of the electioneering canvass then moved quietly on and resulted, as before stated, in the election of the regularly nominated Democratic or Jackson candidates made at the caucus January 8, at Jefferson City.

At the election in August of this year St. Louis county cast 1,830 votes for Governor, which showed the aggregate voters of the county and the claim their numbers gave them on the Post-office Department for a daily mail to St. Louis.

At length it was announced by the mail contractor that from and after the 20th of September, 1836, he would deliver a daily mail at the St. Louis Postoffice.

In the issue of the *Missouri Republican* of the same day it was anounced that from that date there would be a daily issue of that paper, and it has been continued to the present as then announced. It is a part of the history of St. Louis, also, to record that one of the persons who assisted to work off the paper on that day had then been in the office nine years, and continues in it still, and is its principal proprietor in 1870, a period of 43 years.

The year 1836 will ever be memorable with Missourians as the year in which she attained her full growth by the addition of the Indian Reservation (as mentioned in a former chapter), a tract embracing seven of the northwestern counties on the left bank of the Missouri river. To divide this into counties must have been the most pleasant task that Missouri ever imposed on her legislators. It was not a purchase, it was not a trophy; it was a most gracious gift of the most valuable kind. Nothing like it has ever been received by any other State. It was the boon above all others most desirable to Missourians, and appears to have been divided most wisely into counties for convenience and improvement. The legislators of the State never met with more kindly feelings toward each other, although party lines were well defined; public good, however, was the aim of all, and to that they seemed to give their undivided attention.

The progress of the National Road westward had been

virtually suspended, as if awaiting the experiment of the system of railroads. An effort had already been made in the early part of the year to test the views of the wise men of the State, and they had been expressed and promulgated in favor of the system unanimously. Therefore Mr. George K. McGunnegle, who had acted as Secretary to the Railroad Convention and was now a member of the Legislature, drafted a bill to charter a railroad and introduced it into the Legislature in 1836, which was the first step in that direction in Missouri.

The thorough canvass of the State before the election in August, and the published result of that election, had so completely developed the strength of each party that the approaching Presidential election in Missouri excited but little interest in either party, as it was generally conceded that the candidates nominated at Jefferson City on the 8th of January would be elected at the election on the 7th of November, 1836. The Whig party, however, kept up their party organization and polled a respectable minority vote, the result showing George F. Bollinger, John Sappington, William Monroe and Abraham Byrd duly elected Presidential Electors to cast the votes of the State of Missouri on the 6th day of December, 1836. Accordingly, on the 6th day of December, they met at Jefferson City and voted for Martin Van Buren for President and Richard M. Johnson for Vice-President.

The Senators of Missouri in Congress were often congratulated on the happy escape of Missouri from Indian neighbors, and the condition of the people of Missouri contrasted with the people of Florida, who had been long annoyed by the hostile Seminoles.

Among others was the President elect, a few days before his inauguration, to whom Colonel Benton replied: "If the Seminoles had Missourians to deal with their stay would be short in Florida."

Mr. Van Buren asked if Missourians were preferable to regular troops. Mr. Benton gave his reasons for thinking so, and the subject was dropped.

The merchants of St. Louis had enjoyed facilities for the transaction of business equal to those afforded by a bank from the expiration of the charter of the United States Bank of 1816 through the agency of the Commercial Bank of Cincinnati, to whom it had transferred its business in St. Louis on its dissolution.

On the first day of February, 1837, the Legislature of Missouri incorporated "The Bank of the State of Missouri," with a capital of five millions of dollars, and on the same day elected the following named gentlemen officers of the bank: John Smith, President of the parent bank, and Hugh O'Neil, Samuel S. Rayburn, Edward Walsh, Edward Dobyns, William S. Sublette and John O'Fallon, all of St. Louis, directors. A branch was also instituted at Lafayette, and J. J. Lowry was appointed President, W. H. Duncan, J. Villey, Wade M. Jackson and James Erickson, directors.

Soon after the passage of the act chartering the State Bank another act was passed for the exclusion of all bank agencies from the State.

The Bank of the State of Missouri, with its mighty capital of five millions of dollars, commenced operations in a field clear of all competitors and backed by the deposits of the General Government. It soon became the source of business prosperity, but not of reckless extravagance or speculation. Its notes were regarded as equal to the coin their faces represented, and the directory the standard of moral worth in the community in which it acted during its existence as a corporation.

The candidates for President and Vice-President, for whom Missouri's electors had voted, were on examination declared duly elected, and were inaugurated on March 4, 1837, and, as usual on such occasions, the Senators waited a few days to confirm the appointments made by the new President, Missouri's Senators among the rest.

When the press of business incident to such an occasion had subsided, the President called Senator Benton's attention to the remarks he had made in relation to the Florida Indians, and asked if Missourians could be induced to travel so far and assist in chastising them. Colonel Benton answered: "The Missourians will go wherever their services are needed," and went immediately to Mr. Joel R. Poinsett, then Secretary of War, and urged him to issue an order for raising volunteers in Missouri for that purpose. The Secretary being assured of a favorable response, issued an order or requisition on the

Governor of Missouri for two regiments of mounted volunteers for the United States service.

The first regiment was raised and organized by Gen. Richard Gentry, over which he was elected Colonel, John W. Price, Lieutenant-Colonel, and Wm. H. Hughes, Major. Four companies of the second regiment were also raised and organized, and attached to the first regiment.

These troops were presented with a beautiful flag by the ladies of Columbia, and marched from that village on the 6th day of October, 1837, toward the seat of war. They spent a few days at Jefferson Barracks, where they were addressed by Hon. Thos. H. Benton, and then embarked on steamboats and were transported to Jackson Barracks, near New Orleans. Here they were embarked on sailing vessels, to be transported to Tampa Bay, in Florida.

On the voyage they were overtaken by a violent storm and several of the vessels stranded. Many horses were lost but no lives, and they disembarked on the 15th of November at the place of destination. On the 1st of December they received orders from Gen. Zachary Taylor, then commanding in Florida, to march to Okee-cho-bee lake, in the vicinity of which the whole force of the Seminoles was said to have collected, under their four most redoubtable leaders, Sam. Jones, Tiger Tail, Alligator and Mycanopee, prepared for battle.

Having reached the Kessima river, the cavalry scouts captured several Indians who were guarding grazing stock, by which the General learned the Indians were near at hand; and immediately crossing the river, he formed the Missouri volunteers in front and advanced, supporting them at a proper distance by the regular army on either flank.

The Indians appeared to have noticed all the surroundings of the place, and commenced the attack at the point affording them the best position for prolonging a battle, and continued it with a pertinacity they seldom exhibit.

General Gentry fought on foot, as did all his command, and had repulsed the Indians after several hours of severe fighting. He was gradually pushing them across a swamp, and had nearly reached the dry soil, when a bullet pierced his abdomen, inflicting a fatal wound. He knew its extent, yet he stood erect an hour afterward and cheered his men to victory, until at last being compelled to yield, he was borne from the fight and expired the following night.

The fall of their leader did not relax the exertions of the Missourians. They made good all their Senator had said of them, and continued to fight several hours longer, until the Indians were entirely vanquished.

The loss in killed and wounded was one hundred and twelve, most of whom were Missourians.

There being no further service required of the Missourians, they were returned to their homes early in 1838, and the name and fame of General Gentry placed where it will never perish.

A pleasing incident was witnessed by the sick and wounded Missourians on their journey homeward that deserves a place in history, and may be found in the Journals of St. Louis of that date:

After the battle of Okee-cho-bee General Taylor ordered the sick and wounded of his army, in the field-hospital, to be removed to Pensacola for their more comfortable accommodation.

They were conveyed to Tampa Bay and embarked on board a steamboat and arrived near sundown at Pensacola, where the most fashionable people had made preparations for a most splendid ball in honor of the recent victory; and the ladies were making their toilets, preparing for the soiree, when it was announced that the wounded had arrived from the battle field to find hospitals among them.

The ladies, as if by preconcerted arrangement, at once quit their toilets, threw open the doors of their mansions and hastened with their carriages to the steamboat offering their houses for hospitals and themselves as nurses to the sick and wounded.

It is unnecessary to say there was no dancing that evening, but a strife to save what of life remained from the hands of the savages and the more death-bearing miasma of the swamps of Florida.

When the Missourians were able to travel, they parted with their kind benefactors and returned in small squads to their former homes, bearing in their grateful bosoms a lasting remembrance of the kind attentions of the ladies of Pensacola.

CHAPTER XIX.

Visit of Hon. Daniel Webster to St. Louis—Death of Hon. David Barton, one of the First United States Senators from Missouri.

The growth of St. Louis during the last four years of the administration of President Jackson, from January, 1833, to January, 1847, is more readily shown by Mr. John Simond's Harbor Master's report of those two years than any other within reach of the historian, viz.:

	Steamers Engaged.	Tonnage.	Entries.	Wharfage Collected.
1832—	86	9,520	500	$2,567
1836—	144	19,447	1,355	7,138

There was then no hotel, store or saloon within the city west of Fourth street, nor any house more than two stories high. In short, there was such a desideratum experienced by travelers that the citizens felt it their duty to correct it by building more ample hotels, and in 1837 laid the foundation of the Planters' House, but amid the financial disorders of the year very little progress was made.

In the early part of the summer of this year the people of St. Louis were flattered with the hope that they were to be honored by a joint visit of two of the greatest statesmen of the age, Henry Clay and Daniel Webster, whose fame was so wide-spread that their very names were but synonyms for statesmanship and eloquence.

The friends and admirers of both were so numerous here, and their admiration of them so little short of adoration, that it excited a kind of frenzy to see and hear them, and to do them honor.

A public meeting was therefore called to make arrangements to receive the distinguished statesmen as became the people of a great and polished city.

The Hon. Robert Wash, Judge of the Supreme Court, was called to the chair, and resolutions passed that due honors should be paid the distinguished visitors.

Suitable arrangements were made and committees appointed to carry out the resolutions.

Agreeably to the resolutions adopted by the meeting, when it was known that the steamboat on which they were expected to arrive had passed the mouth of the Ohio, the committee proceeded in a steamboat with a number of friends to meet them, which they did at a point below Jefferson Barracks, and being put on board the Robert Morris, the boat expected to bring both statesmen, they met only Mr. Webster; he, however, had his family with him, which partially relieved the disappointment, and the boat proceeded toward the city, where was seen displayed from the flagstaffs of all the steamboats in port, the court-house and town-house, the national flag, and on very many business houses and private mansions a similar emblem, to testify the profound respect entertained for the distinguished visitors.

The Robert Morris passed up the river to near Bremen, to give the visitors an outside view of the city and its commercial operations, and returned to the landing at the foot of Market street, where the guests were welcomed by applauding thousands, and, on their landing, conducted to the National Hotel, now St. Clair Hotel, where they spent several days, and were visited by large numbers of the most distinguished citizens, who vied with each other to make their stay agreeable.

In order to testify the appreciation the Western people entertained of the Eastern statesman and "expounder of the Constitution," and to give all the people a sight of the great patriot and orator, the citizens prepared a sumptuous banquet (in Western parlance, a barbecue or feast) in the field near the spot where Lucas Market now stands, then a beautiful grove of timber of natural growth, belonging to Judge J. B. C. Lucas, in the middle of the present city.

It was summer, but a cloud-shady day and pleasant. Colonel Charles Keemle, as Marshal of the day, assisted by several other gentlemen as deputies, arranged the citizens in a procession, preceded by a choice band of music, and escorted Mr. Webster to the grove, where General William H. Ashley presided as President, and Messrs. Richard Graham, Wm. Carr Lane, John B. Sarpy, John Perry, James Clemens, Jr., and Jas. Russell as Vice-Presidents.

There were five thousand persons present, many of whom were from the surrounding country, attracted hither by the reputation of the great statesmen and a desire to witness his powerful eloquence and gather his political wisdom.

There was a bounteous repast provided of all that usually makes mortals happy, puts them on a par with each other and gives zest to happy feelings and festive enjoyment; nor were they disappointed in their anticipated feast of reason.

When all had sufficiently satisfied the cravings of the body, the great orator arose amid the acclamations of thousands and enchained their rapturous attention for eighty minutes while he defined his own political views and pointed out what he conceived to be the errors of his opponents. He was frequently cheered by the enthusiastic crowd, who in their frenzy seemed desirous of bearing him aloft, if not to the skies, at least as high as their hands could carry him, and were only restrained from attempting it by a desire to have him continue the flood from the same fountain.

As the shades of evening drew near and the labors of the day admonished to rest, the orator was escorted to his lodgings without the least unhappy circumstance occurring to mar the pleasures of the day or lessen its felicity.

This visit of the American statesman attracted the notice of many of the old residents, who had participated in the reception of General Lafayette twelve years before, and led them to contrast the size and appearance of the city at the two periods and the crowds attending the two personages on their reception. The number who attended the statesman's banquet in 1837 were estimated to outnumber the whole population of the city of St. Louis at the time General Lafayette visited them, in 1825.

The financial prospects of St. Louis were never in a more flattering and safe condition than at the time of Mr. Webster's visit to the West; but he had scarcely returned homeward when one of those financial tempests arose among the banks in the Eastern States that, like a tornado, overturned the feeble paper works of irresponsible institutions and even shook and terrified those of the firmest character and induced them to contract the extension of their favors for their own preservation, to the utter ruin of thousands who had relied on their indulgence and were now swept into the vortex of insolvency.

Fortunately for the people of St. Louis and Missouri, it

occurred at a period when the venturesome were waiting for the Bank of the State of Missouri to get into full operation, and there was no other banking institution allowed to operate in the State. Moreover, the old prudent French element had not then entirely departed, and the policy of Jackson's administration to pay debts rather than make them was popular with most of the Board of Directors, who practiced what they taught and had thereby kept their friends aloof from the ruin that at the time overtook and prostrated thousands in other cities. Many persons lost heavily by the general financial crash of that year in St. Louis, yet very few mercantile firms failed, for in those days one merchant sustained another more than at the present time and thus gave themselves a character they long enjoyed.

On the 26th of September, 1837, Hon. David Barton died in Cooper county, at the residence of Mr. Gibson. He had been long a resident of Missouri, was one of her most distinguished statesmen, and presided over the convention that formed the Constitution of Missouri in 1820. He was elected a United States Senator and was the colleague of Col. Thomas H. Benton, having drawn the lot for the four years' term when those two gentlemen took their seats in the United States Senate. He was re-elected and continued in that office to the 4th of March, 1831, when Hon. Alexander Buckner became the colleague of Senator Benton. Mr. Barton was afterward elected to the State Senate from St. Louis county, where he assisted in revising the Statutes of Missouri, as authorized by an act of the Legislature of 1834-5. He was a gentleman of profound learning, legal acquirements and of unquestionable integrity, to which, and his own industry and efforts, he was alone indebted for his great fame and exalted character.

CHAPTER XX.

The First Public School Houses Erected in St. Louis—Death of Rev. E. P. Lovejoy, Late of St. Louis, at Alton, Ills.— Burning of the State House at Jefferson City.

The current of prosperity had flown in such a swift and steady stream in the eastern United States for such a length of time that the people of Missouri appeared to have become emulous of imitating them in as many of their financial schemes as possible in 1837.

They had prepared the way for their enterprise as far as it could be done on paper, and by legislation at the session of 1836-7, with charters for railroads, a bank, chamber of commerce, insurance companies, a medical society, a hotel company and a gaslight company; also an act for building the Capitol at Jefferson City.

The population of St. Louis was then only 16,187, and these schemes were viewed as herculean and visionary by many, yet they have all been accomplished, and others more extensive, useful and brilliant.

The people commenced the year with the most determined energy, and nothing they undertook in that year has failed to be prosecuted to completion, or is still in full and successful growth and progress.

The first and most noteworthy action of that year was the meeting of the St. Louis Public School Board on the 19th of January, 1837, which consisted of M. P. Leduc, A. Gamble, A. Kerr, John Finney and H. L. Hoffman as directors.

There had then been no public school in St. Louis, although the board was organized in April, 1833. It had accumulated a fund of $2,454 45 cash, and held bonds for lots sold amounting to $1,165 17 1-2; and on this small sum it was determined to commence building houses for the use of the public schools, which have since come to be regarded as the most useful and ornamental edifices in the city.

The next remarkable occurrence was the launch of the new steamboat North St. Louis, from the yard of Thomas & Glenn, being the first and most novel thing of the kind, which was witnessed by about one thousand delighted spectators, on the 29th day of March of that year, in the northern part of the city.

Soon after, the Gas Light Company, under the superintendency of M. L. Clarke, S. W. Wilson, J. D. Daggett and J. H. Caldwell, commenced the novel and stupendous project of lighting the city with gas, which, herculean as it was, they accomplished on the 3d of November, 1847, and on that evening illuminated the city for the first time with gas, to the wonder and delight of thousands.

All the other corporations of about the same date began to reap the reward of their labors at a much earlier day, but not without a jar by the financial crash of 1837 that shook them to their centres at the time of its occurrence. The first noticeable sign of the catastrophe was exhibited in St. Louis on the 22d of May, 1837, by the suspension of specie payments at the agency of the Commercial bank of Cincinnati in St. Louis, and the immediate confirmation of the report that all the banks in the city of New York had stopped payment on the 10th of May, but would receive each other's notes at their counters. A few days later President Van Buren's proclamation of May 16, 1837, convening Congress on the first Monday in September, arrived, and by the same mail was received the news of the stoppage of specie payments generally in the United States.

The news seemed not to agitate Missourians much, as they had but little paper money, or, indeed, much of any kind, as the payments for homesteads in those days absorbed all idle dollars in the United States Land offices; and the exports were furs and lead, and could be but little injured in price if all the banks were annihilated and their officers sent to hunting and mining.

Business moved forward as usual, as the Bank of the State of Missouri, on the first of June, five days before, had purchased all the notes of the people in the Commercial Bank of Cincinnati agency on a credit of two years, and it could thereby indulge its friends in the trying crisis without jeopardy, inconvenience or loss, as they paid but five per cent. interest.

Thus Missouri went on as usual without witnessing in her borders any great financial distress or ruin, or suspending any of her public or private enterprises, or having a person idle in her streets or shops. A circular had been received at the St. Louis postoffice on the 24th of May, 1837, from the postmaster general, forbidding the receipt of anything for postage but lawful money of the United States; hence the term "post-office money" (synonym, coin), much used in rustic circles at that period.

On the first Monday of September the twenty-fifth Congress of the United States convened, pursuant to President Van Buren's proclamation of May 15th, in which Missouri was represented in the Senate by Hon. Thomas H. Benton and Hon. Lewis F. Linn, and in the House of Representatives by Albert G. Harrison and John Miller.

All of these gentlemen were regarded as friends of the administration and relied on to act with it in any emergency that might arise in the financial and political strife then existing, which was but little less than civil war.

Missouri then occupied a conspicuous position in the eyes of the nation, and St. Louis a favored point to withstand the financial tempest that was sweeping over the country.

The disbursement of public money through the office of Gen. Clarke, superintendent of Indian affairs, to pay annuities to many tribes of Indians and their agents, placed large sums of money in circulation in the city and State. The payment of the troops engaged on the frontier and disbursements for their supplies and transportation, put other large sums into the hands of the people who furnished them.

Besides these sources, the fur, lead and Santa Fe trade furnished great sums of specie, and thus saved Missouri from the calamities so much complained of in other localities where suspended banks were numerous.

The martial pride of Missourians was incited and somewhat gratified on being alone called on for volunteers at that time to drive the Seminoles out of the swamps of Florida, while others were allowed to stay at home and complain and quarrel over paper money and specie circulars. In the meantime their friends enjoyed the pleasure of seeing them respond to the call with alacrity and perform all the duties assigned them with a promptitude and precision that has covered all the actors engaged in that distant campaign with never-fading glory.

The year 1837 was very remarkable for having such a multiplicity of incidents occurring in Missouri in such quick succession that news gatherers had but little trouble to find items to gratify all appetites for knowledge or novelty, although nothing happened to change the current of human affairs very materially from its accustomed channel.

On Saturday, 1st of July, the private stockholders of the Bank of the State of Missouri elected George K. McGunnegle and Theodore L. McGill directors, and thus completed the full complement of the directory and its entire organization.

It had previously assumed the functions of a bank by using the funds and furniture purchased of the Commercial Bank of Cincinnati, through its agency in St. Louis, and thus entered, without delay, into full operation and usefulness and issued its own notes on the 30th of the same month, and withdrew the others.

The *Missouri Republican* was issued on the morning of the 3d of October, 1837, under the firm of Chambers, Harris & Knapp, to whom it had been sold by Edward Charless and Nathaniel Paschall, who had purchased it of Joseph Charless, the founder and publisher of it under the title of *Missouri Gazette*, in 1808, and continued it under the new name of *Missouri Republican* to that date.

It was the first newspaper ever published on the west bank of the Mississippi, and is the only connected record which historians can refer to with the certainty of obtaining facts on all subjects treated of in a public journal, from the day of its first issue to the present time, 1870.

On the same day, and in the same paper, is the announcement that the St. Louis Theater would open for the first time in the new edifice, at the southeast corner of Third and Olive streets, under the management of Ludlow & Smith, proprietors. The enterprise, like everything else attempted in St. Louis, was a success, but was forced to give place some years after to the more superb edifices for more lucrative employments, and thus the churches, theatres, tombs and grave-yards of that early day, like the mole hills and theatre, have yielded their sites to the mammon of commerce among us.

On the 10th of August of this year Mr. John Shackford, then Sergeant-at-arms of the United States Senate, died in St. Louis, at the residence of his son-in-law, Gen. Nathan Ranney (his former partner under the firm of Shackford & Ranney, wholesale grocers, in the early days of St. Louis steamboating, when they had the only store of the kind at the present Levee).

The name of Mr. Shackford can not be omitted in the history of St. Louis as one of its most enterprising citizens. In the earlier days of commercial enterprise there was no passage over the Ohio falls at Louisville by steamboats for most of the year. This was a great detriment to the public, and none saw or felt it more than Mr. Shackford, and, like a man who attempts the improvement of a highway which he is in constant use of, he stepped forward and took stock in the Louisville canal, to aid the general public and himself. In short, St. Louis was as deeply interested in its success as any other city, and Mr. Shackford had volunteered his aid; and being a gentleman of indomitable energy and perseverance, he quit his occupation in St. Louis to prosecute the completion of the canal with all possible dispatch.

The task was found to be vastly greater than at first estimated for, and as the United States owned a large quantity of the stock, he was obliged to go in person to Washington City to obtain further aid. This he effected, and the Louisville canal was completed, more through the exertions of Mr. Shackford than any other person engaged in that gigantic enterprise.

This made him acquainted with all the members of Congress, and them with his qualifications; therefore, he was elected by the Senate to the office he held at his death. No panegyrist could add to his reputation as a gentleman and a Christian.

The Hon. John F. Darby, on the 31st of October, 1837, resigned the office of Mayor of the city of St. Louis, and on the 15th of November, Dr. Wm. Carr Lane was elected to that office, and, being twice re-elected, he continued in the office until April, 1840.

It has been recorded in a preceding chapter that the office of the St. Louis *Observer*, edited by Rev. Elijah P. Lovejoy, had been broken into and the types scattered in the street. It may, therefore, interest the reader to learn the sequel of that transaction, as it is somewhat connected with the history of St. Louis, and is accordingly given in connection with it. The materials in the office of the *Observer* having been conveyed to Alton, Illinois, Mr. Lovejoy commenced issuing the *Observer* as before, and probably being unreconciled to the ill treatment his press had received in St. Louis, indulged in some remarks that brought dissatisfaction to parties in Alton, who effectually destroyed the press and materials.

Mr. Lovejoy having still some means, and being also well sustained by friends, soon procured another press and materials, and had them stored in Godfrey, Gilman & Co.'s warehouse in Alton, preparatory to recommence issuing.

The destructives and malcontents who had destroyed his first press and threatened violence to future attempts in that direction, having learned the place of deposit, made preparations to demolish the new press, and assembled for that purpose on the night of the 8th of November, 1837, at the warehouse.

In the meantime Mr. Lovejoy and a few friends had armed themselves for the defense of the property, which, however, was destroyed by the mob, Mr. Lovejoy killed and his friends dispersed, while one of the assailants was also killed and several others wounded in the progress of those violent and desperate proceedings.

The State House in Jefferson City took fire on the night of Wednesday, November 17, 1837, and was consumed with all the papers in the office of the Secretary of State, the whole of the furniture of that office and about one-half of the State library, involving a loss that can never be supplied with its original richness. The whole of the accumulations of seventeen years in that important office were thus suddenly swept away, leaving no trace of bonds or original acts signed by the Governors of the State or any officer in the State during the time.

The building was of wood, and was designed to be used as the Governor's residence when the Capitol should be completed, which was then in progress of construction.

The fire is supposed to have originated from a brand rolling out on the floor from the wood fire, which was without a fender in those primeval days of Missouri.

The cost of the house was twelve thousand dollars, and the furniture and library eight thousand more.

This loss in property that might be replaced received no

consideration when contrasted with the public records, bonds and papers destroyed in the office of the State department, which embraced all made during the gubernatorial administrations of Governors McNair, Bates, Miller and Franklin, and a part of Governor Bogg's, that could never be restored.

The historians of Missouri must all rely on other sources of information than the State department for facts prior to the 17th of November, 1837, the date of the conflagration of the State House and papers, in all coming time.

CHAPTER XXI.

The Ice and Frost of 1838—Opening of First Public Schools in St. Louis—Death of Gen. William Clarke, First Governor of the Territory after the Adoption of the Name of Missouri—The Mormons Arrive in Missouri and are Expelled for Misconduct—The Establishment of the St. Louis Criminal Court.

The political elements of Missouri have never required much excitement to put them in motion, and the circumstances that existed at the commencement of 1838 offered an extended field for the display of all the political talent that could be brought into action in the ensuing canvass. There was plenty of talent of the first order in each party and plenty of organs to make that talent and the designs of parties known and appreciated. Those then most widely known and circulated in Missouri as lights and guides to parties were the *Missouri Republican* on the part of the Whigs, and the *Argus* on the part of the Democrats in St. Louis, and the *Missourian*, published at Jefferson City, also Democratic.

These occupied the high ground in the political battle field, while several other lesser lights illuminated the more remote sections of the State with equal brilliancy.

The Democrats, as usual, met at Jefferson City on the 8th of January and nominated John Miller and John Jameson candidates for the Twenty-sixth Congress, who were subsequently elected over Beverly Allen and John Wilson, nominated for the same office, by the Whig party.

The Democratic journal, the *Argus*, a tri-weekly until then, became a daily, and the canvass was conducted with great energy and spirit by both parties to the end of the campaign.

The month of February of 1839 was remarkably cold, the ice being two feet thick on the Missouri river opposite St. Charles, and the heaviest wagons crossed it daily during three consecutive weeks.

The Mississippi was also covered with ice above Bissell's point to its source. It was cleared of ice so as not to obstruct the St. Louis ferry opposite the city, but was closed below at the Big Muddy, and navigation was suspended during three weeks of February of that year.

It was so intensely cold in St. Louis that the Young Men's Political Society, on the 24th of February, adjourned for one week, on account of the excessive inclemency of the weather, which was equally severe through the whole State and territories westward.

The St. Louis public schools made their first practical essay this year with great success, and have nearly kept pace in growth with the improvements and population of the city since, without a serious accident or loss by fire or storm to this time, 1870.

A general spirit of literary enterprise seemed to be awakened that year, and several wealthy gentlemen urged forward private schools of a high grade. Messrs. Moure and Wyman among the first, each established one of that kind, which flourished many years.

Kemper College was opened under the auspices of the Episcopalians and Drs. Hall and McDowell.

Dr. Joseph N. McDowell commenced the labors that deservedly connect his name with the history of St. Louis as one of its most distinguished and useful citizens on the first day of September, 1839, by lecturing on the natural history of man, and elucidated his theory by exhibiting skulls of several different races of men, and pointing out to his auditory the marked difference apparent in their forms, and then explained the characteristics peculiar to each race.

This lecture brought him at once into notice as one connected in the Kemper College enterprise, and he immediately commenced the erection of a brick edifice for a medical college connected with Kemper College, a short distance westwardly from the site of that well known stupendous edifice he erected some years after, when he found his first establishment entirely too small to accommodate the large number of students who flocked to him for instruction, and which has yet, and probably always will, bear the name of its founder—"McDowell's College"—until some sad catastrophe destroys it.

On the same evening that Dr. McDowell delivered his first lecture in St. Louis, Governor William Clarke died, at the age of sixty-eight years, in the city where he had long resided. He had been closely connected with the interests of Missouri and its history for thirty-four years, and was more extensively known then to red and white men than any man had ever been before, and had more influence over the red men than any one else has ever possessed.

He was known and respected by all the Indian nations, however remote, untutored, coy or timorous, and beloved and followed in his advice as an oracle or a deity, from the distant shores of the Pacific to his own hearthstone, on the bank of the Mississippi.

He was the first governor of the territory of Missouri after the adoption of its new name, and subsequently superintendent of Indian Affairs of the western division to his death. After his death St. Louis was no longer the Mecca to red men; their annual visits ceased, and the familiar sights of groups of rich, fantastically-dressed, painted Indians were no longer seen in the streets, surrounded by troops of children admiring their costumes, witnessing their dances, and listening to their rude music. Their friend and benefactor, their guide and adviser, was no more. St. Louis was thereafter but as his tomb to them, and had no longer any charms to attract them hither.

When the general excitement of the election had passed away, 40,618 votes were shown to have been polled in this year for congressmen, while 27,372 only had been polled for governor in 1830, showing the rapid growth of population during the two years just elapsed. Soon after the election two new sources of excitement began to agitate the people in the northern part of the State and urge them to call on the Executive for aid. The first was for protection against the territorial authorities of Iowa, who claimed jurisdiction over a strip of Missouri about six miles wide south of the line of the territory, and attempted to use force to maintain it. This dispute with Iowa was settled peaceably soon after. The second was much more serious, and had more martial, tragic and violent incidents connected with it in its progress.

The Mormons, in great numbers, had arrived in Missouri from Ohio and located themselves as best they could in and about Daviess county, intending to make it their permanent home, without changing their morals or manners from what they were while residing in the neighboring State of Illinois. Their lawlessness soon became unbearable, as they set aside the process of ordinary law and abused its officers. Justice Adam Black, of Daviess county, made an affidavit of their acts on the 9th of August, and called for military assistance. Capt. Bogard responded to the call and went on duty with his company as a posse comitatus. He was surprised and had ten killed and thirty wounded and taken prisoners by the Mormons, who had four hundred men under arms. The governor then called out twenty-five hundred militia, by which the Mormons were arrested, thirty killed, among them two children, and many other acts of great violence done by both parties which can never be justified by a Christian people.

At length peace was restored by force of arms, but no harmony, for Missourians had shown they would not tolerate such unworthy people or permit them to remain in their midst. Therefore the Mormons prepared to leave—not in as limited time as when they came among the Missourians, but with as universal consent as when they left Illinois.

Kemper College was opened on the 15th of October, 1838, under the superintendence of Rev. P. R. Minard, with a board of trustees, seventeen in number, selected from the most learned wealthy, and influential gentlemen of the Protestant Episcopal community in St. Louis, and plenty of students entered.

The St. Louis University was then, as it always has been, in successful, silent progress since it introduction into the city, inciting all others to perseverance, industry and excellence, and, as it gathered strength, adding new facilities to its accumulations for accomplishingh perfection.

The same may be said of the female institution known as the Convent of the Sacred Heart, founded by the munificence of the late John Mullanphy, and conducted much on the same charitable and economical principle—receiving payment of those able to pay and teaching the indigent gratis.

In these two institutions the highest as well as the lowest branches of a finished education have been constantly taught in English, Spanish, French and German by competent instructors in their native language without the least apparent change, except their constant and steady growth and enlargement.

The example and success of these institutions prompted clergymen and laymen to open and patronize Parochial Schools, chiefly Catholics and Episcopalians, which, together with the Public Schools, have since that year been in rapid and constant growth, and have given the people of St. Louis better facilities for educating their children agreeably to their own taste than any other city in the United States.

The date, therefore, of the rapid growth of literary excellence in Missouri coincides with the opening of the St. Louis Public Schools, in 1838, and its progress has been as steadily on the increase as the population of the city since that period.

On the 20th of November of this year the Legislature met at Jefferson City and continued its session until February of 1839, during which many necessary and useful acts were passed, one of which was the establishment of the St. Louis Criminal Court, over which Hon. James B. Bowlin presided as judge several years. Also, an act incorporating the company which built the Planters' House. A Mayor's Court was also instituted. An edifice known as Christ Church, at the southwest corner of Chesnut and Fifth streets, was built and dedicated this year, but which, like the theater, gave place in a few years to commerce, and, assuming vastly greater dimensions, has risen in splendor at a more quiet and retired location, near Lucas Place, corner of Thirteenth and Locust streets.

Financial affairs had assumed (outside of Missouri) a very doubtful aspect, and the officers of the Bank of the State of Missouri observing it, and being determined to protect their bank from loss, refused to receive any suspended bank notes on deposit or in payment at their counter.

This was a distressing movement to the mercantile part of the community at the time, who made an effort to get the resolution rescinded by giving ten of the most responsible gentlemen of the city as indemnificators against loss to the bank. After very deliberate consultation, the directory declined to rescind the resolution. A most violent tempest of words in business circles immediately followed. An indignation meeting was announced and held to express the sentiments of those interested against the directors, and at a later day a counter meeting of friends was held to approve their action, while the bank proceeded as usual, according to the resolution of the directory first published. Very few persons withdrew their deposits from the bank or their business, and it was observable that those who made most noise on either side had no deposits of great magnitude in any bank.

The wisdom of the directory became apparent soon after, and the proffered bondsmen rejoiced in their happy escape from great losses. The bank maintained its credit to the end of a brilliant career, and returned to the stockholders their investments and a fair dividend for its use and risk during the period.

Political meetings in anticipation of the Presidential election of 1840 began to be of frequent occurrence, and halls and places were fitted up for such meetings, and became established as headquarters and received their appropriate names according to the taste of the occupants.

A political organization was formed called the Whig Vigilance Committee, who were very active in keeping their adherents well informed on all political movements and in the strict line of obedience to all the tactics of their party.

It was composed of a very large number of our oldest, youngest and most worthy citizens, and so numerous that it seemed to include nearly every legal voter in the county of that party, which was then in the majority.

The meetings and movements of that association filled the city with more noise and political strife (but without bloodshed) than any other exciting cause (before or since the civil war) has ever done. Their proceedings then distinguished the year 1840 as one of most remarkable political excitement, such as parades, processions, log cabin barbecues and stump speeches.

Notwithstanding the excitement, the impediments and prognostications of disaster to commerce, the march of St. Louis was onward.

There were two thousand and ninety-five arrivals of steamboats reported at the wharf of St. Louis during the year 1839, and a similar prosperity was apparent all over the State.

In April, 1840, the foundation of St. Xavier's Catholic Church, at the corner of Ninth and Green streets, attached to the St. Louis University, was laid with the usual ceremonies observed on such occasions, in presence of a large concourse of spectators. It was the second edifice of the kind built and now standing in the city, and was the most western at that time, and was located beyond the limits of the corporation. Thirty years have scarce elapsed since, and the edifice is now in the middle of a city fifteen times as large and containing fifteen times as many inhabitants as at that period.

On the first Monday of April of this year Hon. John F. Darby was elected Mayor of the city, an office he had resigned two or three years previously, when his term of office had only about half expired. It was regarded as a political triumph on the part of the Whigs, as disclosing their reliable strength in the city at the polls and the certainty of future success.

CHAPTER XXII.

Establishment of the Ten Hour System of Labor — Great Extension of the City Limits and Division into Five Wards — The Abolition of Property Qualifications for Voters — The Murder of Two Young Men by Four Negroes, and their subsequent Arrest, Conviction and Execution.

The success of the Whigs at the municipal election in April intensified their exertions to gain the State of Missouri, and Messrs. Nathaniel Paschall and Charles G. Ramsey came into the political field as auxiliaries at about the same time, with powerful pens and good presses, under the name and style of

The New Era, and did honor to the cause they had espoused to the end of the canvass, as well as assisted in elevating the commercial and literary character of the city and the State.

The ambition to build up the city was not abated or diverted by the political breezes then in lively motion, but a more systematic and less tedious mode of accomplishing it was at this time suggested, considered, and soon after generally adopted. It had been customary, previous to May, 1840, in St. Louis and Missouri, for mechanics and laborers to be present and labor for their employers from sunrise to sunset, taking a recess of one hour from six o'clock to seven A. M., to breakfast, and from twelve o'clock M. to one o'clock P. M. to dine.

About the middle of May of this year several bricklayers asked their employers to establish a fixed number of hours for a day's labor for them, and make it uniform at all seasons of the year. The employers declined to listen to the proposition or fix on ten hours as a day's labor, and the journeymen quit work at once and marched quietly through the principal streets in the order of a procession, to exhibit their numbers, and appointed a public meeting to be held at the court house on the afternoon of the 23d of May, at which a great number of mechanics of all trades attended.

The meeting had been called by the journeymen bricklayers, but the multitude present was composed of a large portion of every mechanical art in operation in the city, and the well-informed, influential citizens.

On the meeting being called to order, Col. Thornton Grimsley was elected chairman, and on his taking his seat expressed his profound sensibility of the high honor that had been conferred on him by being called to preside over a journeymen's meeting, and declared he would try to discharge the duties as far as he was able; that he was not a bricklayer, but a saddle and harness maker, and employed many journeymen, and, from interested motives, might be supposed to be opposed to their movements. He, however, assured them he was not, but approved of the measure as reasonable and just. Then, turning around and viewing his auditory, he said: "I see many employers of journeymen before me of other trades, who, if they come into this ten-hour system, may in some instances lose a little time of painful toil, but will be well rewarded for the sacrifice in better, willing labor, and enjoy the smiles of wives and little children at the early return of their husbands and fathers from labor if they will go and see them meet." The sequel was, the ten-hour system was adopted, and has prevailed these thirty years since without discord or dissent among all classes who labor by the day or employ others to labor for them.

The quadrennial election was drawing near, and large meetings of the Whigs were held throughout the city, usually one each evening at a point remote from the place of the last meeting, at which large numbers from distant sections of the city convened, marching in open order to give apparent importance to the meeting and *eclat* to their movements. Thus most of the evenings of June and July, 1840, were spent interspersed with songs, shouts, huzzas and shows as variable as ingenuity and enthusiasm could invent or money purchase. In the meantime, their Democratic brethren looked on in amusement at their devices to win converts to their cause, and with equal vigilance and pertinacity, but with silence and caution, watched their lines and exhorted to constancy and perseverance, and in the State held the reins of power. At length the votes were cast and counted, when it was found 29,625 votes had been given for Thomas Reynolds for governor, and 22,212 for John B. Clark; therefore Thos. Reynolds was elected governor by a majority of 7,413 of the whole 51,837 votes which had been given for governor in 1840, after the most unusual activity had been exerted by both parties to bring their whole strength to the polls.

M. M. Marmaduke was elected lieutenant-governor at the same time. John Miller and John C. Edwards were also elected members of Congress, with a majority of about seven thousand votes each over their Whig competitors.

The Democratic party had elected a decided majority of the members of the Legislature of 1840. The St. Louis county delegation, however, was Whig, and, therefore, could hope to have but a feeble voice in the future political movements of the Legislature.

The Whigs of St. Louis still hoped Missouri would cast her four votes for Harrison, the Whig candidate for the Presidency, and continued their exertions and organizations until after the presidential election in November, when the Democratic nominees were elected in Missouri, and cast the vote of the State for Martin Van Buren.

The Legislature met on the 21st of November, and about that time it was ascertained that a majority of the electors chosen in the United States were Whigs. The elation of the Whigs at this announcement surpassed anything of the kind ever witnessed before in the city.

The St. Louis theatre was offered by the proprietor for an Athenæum for an oration, which was delivered by Hon. Wilson Primm, then one of the youngest members of the St. Louis bar. Col. John O'Fallon presided as president of the meeting, assisted by several vice-presidents.

The whigs devoted the day to the jubilee, and if the rolling of the stone of Sysiphus did not cease, the issue of the *Missouri Republican* did, which demonstrated the devotion of that sheet to the cause it had espoused.

All mechanical professions were represented in a grand procession, which moved in triumph through the principal streets of the city in the early part of the day, exhibiting every demonstration of joy and gladness.

In the early part of this year the palatial steamer Meteor made the trip from New Orleans to St. Louis in five days and five hours, being the quickest trip ever made from that port before that time.

The political excitement of the period seemed to arouse the energies of the aged and cause them to act the part of youth, and prompted youth to act the part of manhood so far that although the politicians contrived to engross much of the time of their constituents in political enterprises, the progress of business advanced with as much activity and regularity as in quiet times, and the current of business and growth of the city advanced with its usual velocity, if not regularity, and banished ennui and suicides from the heads of all politicians.

The Missouri Legislature was industriously engaged in framing laws for improving the State, incorporating new towns and villages, companies of insurance and others, locating State roads, forming new counties, changing the lines of others, and fixing county seats for all not established.

The rapid growth of St. Louis engaged their careful attention, and on the 4th of January, 1841, the Legislature extended the city limits on the south, the west, and the north very considerably, as follows: "Beginning at a point due east of the southeast corner of St. George Addition, thence westwardly to second Carondelet Avenue, thence with west line of said Avenue to the north line of Chouteau Avenue, thence to the mouth of Stony Creek, thence by the line of the river to the place of beginning."

The Mayor and Board of Aldermen were authorized to divide the city into five wards and make other municipal regulations with enlarged powers, greatly to the advancement of permanent improvements within the city limits.

The most noteworthy act, however, of that Legislature was the abolition of property qualifications for voters and municipal officers, which was passed at that session.

On the 8th of February, Hon. Luke E. Lawless, then Judge of the Circuit Court of St. Louis County, adjourned the court to the 18th inst., as he was certain that during this short time he would be re-appointed to that office and be confirmed by the Senate, and thus be enabled to remount the judicial bench, elated in view of his haters, or some other person would be appointed, confirmed, and perhaps qualified to take the seat, and thereby he would save himself from the contemptuous grin that would display itself if the announcement should arrive while he was actually sitting on the bench.

The well-timed act saved him from the evils of the latter alternative. Before the adjournment elapsed the governor appointed Hon. Bryan Mullanphy to the office, who was confirmed by the Senate, and he entered on the discharge of the duties of the office, while Judge Lawless retired quietly to private life in the city.

The well known and well built Planters' House was opened by Messrs. Stickney & Knight as proprietors on the first day of April, 1841, and dinner was served there on that day for the first time; and it has been kept open in the same style during the twenty-nine years since, and is at this day a model house for all the world, being large, convenient, central, well lighted and airy, with access, ingress and egress easy from all points and occupying a most healthful elevation.

At the municipal election in April, 1841, Hon. John D. Daggett was elected mayor of the city and was installed into office as usual in such cases. The public excitement seemed quieted and the current of business taking its proper channel when, on the morning of the 18th of April, the citizens were roused by the cry of fire, and the firemen turned out with alacrity and proceeded to the east end of Pine street, where a large stone warehouse was on fire, occupied in front by Simonds & Morrison and in the rear by Wm. G. Pettus as a broker's office.

The fire appearing general and the doors being closed, they were broken open and Jacob Weaver found murdered, lying on the floor in a pool of his own blood. The whole building was on fire inside, and the adjacent building ignited and others in danger. No time was lost by the firemen; they commenced at once to confine the fire to the building already ruined, and while Mr. Ansel S. Kemball, 1st engineer of the Union Fire company, was engaged directing a stream of water on the fire, a portion of the wall fell and instantly killed him. After the building was destroyed the remains of Mr. Jesse Baker were found in the ruins, who had also been murdered and the building fired to conceal the crime. It was subsequently found that both these young men had been murdered by four negroes to rob Mr. Pettus of his money, which they failed to obtain. They were all caught, all convicted, all confessed their guilt, and all were executed at the same time by being hanged on the same beam in presence of thousands of spectators, on an island in the Mississippi in front of the city. This wholesale execution formed another epoch in St. Louis, and the expression, "since the negroes were hung" has not become entirely obsolete among the lads of St. Louis at this distant day.

CHAPTER XXIII.

The Establishment of the Court of Common Pleas—The Appearance of the Native American Party—The Death of Hon. John B. C. Lucas.

The growth of St. Louis and Missouri in population and wealth has long been well shown by its commercial growth. This has been readily ascertained from the Harbor Master's report at the close of each year. His report of steamboat arrivals in 1840 shows that there were 1,721 arrivals, with a tonnage of 244,185, against 1,476 arrivals and 218,103 tonnage in 1839.

The manufacture of flour, as shown by the inspector's report, was 19,075 bbls. in 1840, when only 9,300 were inspected in 1839; 18,056 bbls. of whisky were inspected in 1840, against 13,736 bbls. in 1839. The inspection of beef began to be reported in 1840, and 1,075 bbls. were inspected in that year in St. Louis. Stone coal had come into general use as fuel, and 7,040 wagon and 2,342 cart loads were weighed at the scales in 1840.

In January, 1841, the Legislature established the Court of Common Pleas in St. Louis county, and Judge P. H. Engle, a learned and popular gentleman, presided over it until his declining health forced him from the bench. On the 23d of February of this year the St. Louis Medical School first conferred degrees on its students.

A new party had made its appearance in other cities, and its friends were emulous that St. Louis should distinguish itself under the name of the Native American party also, and, having provided a press to disseminate their principles, they unfurled their partisan banner, under the name of the *Pennant*, and about the 1st of March, 1841, began to publish the outlines of their platform, but studiously withheld the inner lines, except to the initiated, who were born in the United States, for all others were rejected from membership among them.

The Inauguration of President Harrison, on the 4th of March, gave vivacity to politicians at the time and caused some rejoicing among the vehement Whigs of the period; but a sad cloud hung over the future prospects of the party in the shape of a nomination made by the Native American party, in which some Democrats seemed willing to coalesce and share the spoils with them, and thus abated their ardor in all political movements at the municipal election.

However, Hon. John D. Daggett was elected Mayor by the Whigs, who, as a party, governed the city, which then contained 20,504 inhabitants in the old limits at that period. On the day following the election the message of President Harrison arrived, issued on the 20th of March, convening Congress on the 31st of May, 1841, and on the 13th the news of his death, on the morning of the 4th of April, arrived, nine days after the melancholy event.

It is difficult to realize at this day that the news of so important an event at that time traveled so slowly, yet it was then considered a rapid movement of news. The obsequies of President Harrison were solemnized in an appropriate manner on the 22d of April, in which all the people seemed to take a deep interest and to realize the uncertainty and mutability of all human affairs.

No year had witnessed so many changes as this at that time, and each day seemed to promise some extraordinary event to fill the streets with news bearers and willing bearers of the latest wonders.

The steamer Missouri arrived on the 4th of May, from New Orleans, in four days and twenty-three hours from port to to port, being the quickest trip that had ever been made.

Business was steady but not very brisk, as many people were waiting for Congress to create a bank to stimulate commercial action; but Missouri's delegation in Congress opposed the measure as fraught with danger and trouble, and thus kept her friends from the irritation and anxiety that destroyed the comfort and happiness of many who were expecting favors and facilities from sources that could only disappoint or mislead them.

Congress convened in obedience to President Harrison's proclamation, and continued in session until the 13th of September, 1841, engaged most of the time on two fiscal bills, both of which President Tyler vetoed and brought on himself the anathemas of all the Whig Congressmen and the general contempt of his whole party and most of his opponents. His conduct affected Missouri less than any of the other States of equal size, as she was less interested in banking facilities in her commercial transactions.

There were ten insurance companies then in St. Louis, which engaged in banking as far as their capital enabled them, and thus afforded facilities for commercial transactions, in a safe and legitimate way, equal to the wants of a prudent people.

The city having been very considerably enlarged by a legislative act, was divided into five wards, and the street improvements were greatly extended, in addition to the immense enhancement of the value of property in her new limits.

At the municipal election in April, 1842, Hon. Geo. Maguire was elected Mayor of the city, and discharged the duties of the office with such quietude and satisfaction to the people that all seemed to act in harmony with his pacific disposition.

On the 10th of May of this year the corner-stone of the Centenary Church was laid, at the southwest corner of Pine and Fifth streets, where it has stood and been used as a Methodist Episcopal Church for twenty-eight years, and now, in 1870, is converted into a great commercial house and made one of the great centers of trade in the city, while the congregation has built a more imposing structure for their accommodation in a more retired and more suitable location, in an elevated part of the city, westwardly.

In the autumn of 1842 Hon. John B. C. Lucas died. He had been one of the earliest settlers in Missouri, and held the office of Judge of the highest tribunal of the District of Louisiana by appointment from President Jefferson, and continued in that position until the Territory became a State. He had also been appointed a commissioner by Mr. Jefferson to settle the land claims of Upper Louisiana, and held the office until 1812. He was a gentleman of undoubted probity and honor, and most untiring industry and perseverance. Few men in the world ever left more lasting traces of their industry, judgment and character than he.

CHAPTER XXIV.

St. Louis Becomes a Manufacturing City—Remarkable Trial of a Circuit Court Judge before a Criminal Court, and his Acquittal—Change in the Manner of Voting in St. Louis County—The Steamer Edna Collapses a Flue and Destroys the Lives of Fifty-five Persons—The Death of Several Prominent Citizens.

St. Louis had already become a manufacturing city in 1842, and had arrived at it by slow advances and the industry of her own people. No large capitalists had then brought their wealth on this side of the Mississippi to establish factories. They had been built up generally from small beginnings by the persons who then conducted them, some of which continued many years as noble monuments of the untiring industry and perseverance of their builders.

Perhaps no more remarkable instance of this kind can be pointed out than that of Samuel Gaty, Esq., who, in 1829, established himself on the same ground which he occupied with others as an iron foundry, and continued it above thirty years without any change, except perfecting and enlarging it, until all connected with it had acquired princely estates and could retire and enjoy it as best suited their tastes and inclinations.

His example and success prompted others to enter into similar establishments; and the facilities for obtaining coal and iron encouraged the multiplication of foundries for the manufacture of all kinds of castings and machinery in general use.

On the 25th of April of this year the St. Louis Oak came down from the boat-yard of Capt. Irvine, under her enterprising owner and commander Capt. F. Coonce, and was placed at the wharf to receive freight for Galena, for which trade she had been built; and is believed to have been the first boat, with all her engines, tackle and machinery, built entirely in St. Louis.

Her engines and machinery were manufactured by Messrs. Gaty, McCune & Glasby, and their high finish and perfection established the character of that class of manufactures which they have since so eminently maintained in St. Louis and Missouri.

From this period may be dated the growth of boat-building and repairing in and about St. Louis, which has continued without a check; and no disaster of great magnitude has ever occurred in that line without its being covered by insurance.

A most uncommon presentment by the grand jury was made at the May term of this year in the St. Louis Criminal Court against Hon. Bryan Mullanphy, judge of the Circuit Court, for oppression in the discharge of the duties of his office, and he was arraigned for trial on the 10th day of May of that remarkable year.

Such an extraordinary case excited great attention and brought a crowded audience to the court house to hear the accusation and the defense of such a distinguished individual.

The whole occurrence that produced the presentment had transpired in open court in presence of a learned bar of very considerable numbers, and the complainant was one of the number and a gentleman of fine abilities, and was regarded as a profound scholar in the law by most of his associates.

The act, or rather acts, complained of, as shown on the trial, was that, in the progress of a suit in the circuit court, where Judge Mullanphy presided, Ferdinand W. Risque, Esq., who represented one of the parties litigant, had a motion before the court on which the gist of the action rested, and having made a speech before his honor, seemed to expect a decision from the court in his favor. The court, however, delivered a decision which was directly opposite to Mr. Risque's interest and proposition. Thereupon Mr. Risque, casting a most scornful glance at the judge, began snatching up the papers in the case in a contemptuous manner, which the judge could not fail to recognize as directed at him, and ordered Mr. Risque to take his *seat*.

Mr. Risque replied, *I prefer to stand*. Judge Mullanphy then instructed the clerk to enter a fine of fifty dollars against Mr. Risque, and directing his attention again to Mr. Risque, ordered him to take a *seat*. Mr. Risque replied as before, and the judge ordered the clerk to enter another fine of fifty dollars against Mr. Risque, who still remained standing, probably two minutes, when the judge addressed him as before—Mr. Risque, take your *seat*. Mr. Risque replied, *I prefer to stand*, and still remained standing. Judge Mullanphy then ordered the clerk to enter another fine of fifty dollars against Mr. Risque for contempt of court. The judge then ordered the sheriff to remove Mr. Risque from the court room, and business proceeded as usual, Mr. Risque, in the meantime, in charge of the sheriff, leaving the court room.

The whole proceedings and trial were conducted with great ability and decorum, and ended by the jury declaring the judge *not guilty*. More than a quarter of a century has since passed, and most of the actors are dead, but the example lives as a lasting monument that the dignity of courts is not to be trifled with in our community by dissatisfied litigants or their agents.

The public schools of St. Louis had now become well established and popular, but had only two school houses—one on Fourth street, with two teachers, and one on Sixth street, with four teachers. Their salaries were low: one male teacher received $900 per annum, and two male teachers received $500 each per annum. One female teacher received $500 per annum, and two female teachers $400 each per annum.

The first introductory lecture to the summer course of the medical department of the St. Louis University was delivered by Prof. Hall to the students and a crowded auditory on the 28th of March, 1842.

The people of St. Louis had become accustomed to financial troubles, but they were now called on to meet a more general failure of all confidence in banks and paper promises than ever, in the spring of this year.

The notes of the State Bank of Illinois were refused by all the brokers in the city, and St. Louis city warrants were unsaleable at less than fifteen per cent. discount among the people.

The Bank of the State of Missouri refused all notes but its own, which, with the tardy action Congress in furnishing funds for the Indian department and other engagements of the West, had the effect to depress business more during that year than any one in the twenty years preceding.

The apportionment of representation in Congress under the late census of 1840 was delayed until late in May of 1842; and the act then had been so framed that when it was received there was much difficulty in determining what it would be proper to do at the approaching election, as the State had not been divided into districts corresponding in number with her present apportionment.

The election, however, was ordered under the former general ticket system, and every preparation made to verify the strength of parties on the Congressional ticket as usual.

On the 22d of June Hon. James B. Bowlin resigned his office as judge of the Criminal Court of St. Louis county, and a few days after Gov. Thomas Reynolds appointed Alonzo W. Manning, Esq., to the vacant seat.

Judge Bowlin then became a candidate for Congress, and was elected, with James M. Hughes, Jas. H. Relfe, Gustavus B. Bower and John Jameson as his colleagues, at the election in August, 1842.

On the 30th of September, John Smith, president of the Bank of the State of Missouri, resigned that office, which he had held from the founding of that institution with general approbation. The reason he assigned for the act was the inadequacy of his salary to the support of his family and his desire to enter into a more productive employment.

The Legislature convened on the 21st of November, organized, and received the Governor's message on the following day.

After the committee had been formed and all in order for legislation, on the 23d of November the two houses met and re-elected Dr. Lewis F. Linn United States Senator from Missouri.

One of the first and most remarkable acts of this Legislature was the act changing the time and manner of voting in the county and city of St. Louis, which still obtains.

According to the old law the voting was done in two or three days, as directed by the county court, and *viva voce*.

The new act reduced the time to a single day and changed the *viva voce* to voting by ballot. The act was approved by the governor on the 17th of December, 1842, and has now been in operation 27 years.

Five hundred and twenty-five thousand bushels of coal were reported weighed at the different St. Louis scales in 1841, which showed the importance of the trade at that early day, and the progress that was being made in developing the resources of the country.

On taking a retrospective view of the events of this year the most remarkable feature that presents itself to the eye is the frequency of occurrences of a mournful character.

The death of Hon. John B. C. Lucas, on the 20th of August of this year, and his distinguished character and services, have already been noted; and it is left for others at a later day to do justice to his memory, when the extent of the vision of his farseeing eyes into the future greatness of St. Louis shall have become more thoughtfully considered and better known to the thousands dwelling in their palatial residences, on the very grounds he had reclaimed from a state of nature and mowed and plowed over in his declining years, while contemplating the mighty changes he saw so rapidly approaching, and verifying his early predictions.

The arrival of foreigners at St. Louis, and their immediate departure during the spring and summer to the interior, had become so frequent and common that little attention was given to it until Sunday morning, the 3d of July, when one of those appalling catastrophes transpired which shook society by their recital and filled many bosoms with grief by their consequences.

The steamer Edna, a Missouri river boat, had left St. Louis the evening preceding, with about one hundred persons on board, a large portion of whom were German emigrants seeking new homes in the interior of Missouri, at which they had nearly arrived.

The boat had landed in the night near the mouth of the Missouri to wait for daylight to enter the river. The deck passengers, as usual on a crowded boat, had disposed of themselves as best they could in rear of the boilers and engines for sleep, and spent the night quietly.

At dawn of day the assistant engineer made preparations to start, and did start the engine; but before the wheel had made a revolution the two flues of the larboard boiler collapsed, throwing the whole contents of the boiler on the unfortunate sleeping deck passengers, killing the engineer, and producing a scene of horror and distress that is more easily imagined than described.

The steamers Iatan and Annawan were under way, in sight, and their officers came immediately to the assistance of the sufferers, and taking the boat in tow landed it at the St. Louis wharf, when the dead, the dying and the wounded were immediately transferred to the Sisters' Hospital, where they received all the attention that humanity could afford and all the consolation that piety can contribute in such indescribable sufferings.

Fifty-five persons lost their lives by this sad calamity, most of whom were buried from the court house on the next day, the 4th of July, by the citizens, while the city was filled with sorrow and pity for the surviving sufferers.

Eight of the wounded, after great suffering, finally recovered.

St. Louis had but recently followed to the tomb two distinguished individuals, as unlike each other as any two who could be named, and yet both known, beloved and respected by nearly every member of the community.

The first was Mr. Antoine Chenie, a man of peace and quietude. He was born in Montreal, Canada, on the 14th of April, 1768, and died in his well known mansion, on the north side of Market street, May 20, 1842. He had formerly kept a bakery, without a competitor, when the city was in its infancy, and there was not one brick upon another in the form of a human habitation in the county of St. Louis. He had acquired a competency many years before his death, had educated his family and seen them enter life in connection with the most prominent families in the city of their birth.

The other gentleman was Gen. Henry Atkinson, who died on the 15th day of June, 1842. He had early given himself to the profession of arms, had served during the war of 1812 and in the Black Hawk war with great credit and distinction, and had endeared himself to all his brother officers and soldiers at Jefferson Barracks, where he commanded, by his kindness and soldierly bearing, and to the whole community where he dwelt by his urbanity and hospitable disposition.

His obsequies were celebrated under the Rev. Mr. Hedges, chaplain of the post of Jefferson Barracks, and his remains buried with the honors of war in the cemetery at that post.

The distress of the community was not confined to ordinary causes of grief and calamities. On the night of the 10th of August five persons went to the residence of Maj. Floyd, a quiet citizen, near the Fair grounds, and barbarously murdered him by beating him to death, and then robbed his house of a large sum of money in presence of his distressed wife. Several persons were arrested, one was tried and executed, and the other four escaped after many efforts to apprehend and punish them.

On the 19th of September the citizens of St. Louis were called to lament the death of Col. Joseph C. Laveille, one of its most distinguished members, and one of its earliest and greatest builders and promoters—a real, practical and educated mechanic of taste and judgment, who had qualified his mind by profound study to lead those around him in the paths of wisdom and virtue.

He was the first architect of the present St. Louis court house, commenced in 1826, and although more than five times as large now as when it was declared finished by him and his partner, Mr. George Morton, its symmetry and perfection were as creditable to the first architects as the last, in the estimation of connoiseurs.

Joseph W. Walsh, Esq., clerk of the court of common pleas, had held that office from the organization of the court until his death, about the last of September, 1842. He was a most amiable man and a fine scholar, having received his education in St. Louis, and was known to almost every individual in the county who always placed the most implicit confidence in his integrity and honor, and favored him with any office he desired within their gift until his death.

On his demise, Judge Engle appointed John Smith, Esq., late president of the Bank of the State of Missouri, to the vacant clerkship.

He was an old resident of St. Louis, whose probity and honor had been tested in the high position he had occupied in the Bank of the State of Missouri, and hence his appointment to that office gave universal satisfaction. He afterwards became the collector of the taxes of St. Louis county, all of which offices he discharged with the same brilliant fidelity.

CHAPTER XXV.

Remarkable Visit of Audubon, the Ornithologist, to the Mouth of the Yellowstone river, and his safe Return—The Murder and Robbery of Don Chavis on the Santa Fe Road—Visit of Colonel Richard M. Johnson to St. Louis—Death of Maj. Pilcher at St. Louis.

The financial gloom that had operated against the growth of the city seemed to be removed early in the spring of 1843, and more glittering prospects were visible in every branch of business. All classes had become accustomed to relying on industry and economy for progress and prosperity, and less on banks and political movements.

St. Louis had become a great exporting as well as importing city, and relied on specie as a circulating medium of exchange in all commercial transactions.

Prices of all exports were low, but industry and abundant crops had filled the warehouses to overflowing with the productions of 1842, and commercial intercourse was being extended on all the streams tributary to the Mississippi, which caused great activity along the levee and among the steamboats and mechanical work shops.

The prices current in March of that year were: For flour at city mills, $4 to $4 25 per barrel; from country mills, $3 75 per bbl.; wheat 55 to 60 cents per bushel; corn 20 to 22c.; whisky 17c. per gallon; bacon shoulders $1 50 per cwt.; hams $2 50, and sides $3 per cwt.; lard 5 to 5 1-2c. per lb.; lead $2 62 1-2 to $2 68 per cwt.; G. A. salt $1 75 per sack, and L. B. salt $2 25 per sack. The State tobacco warehouse was then being built, also sixty stores, mostly along Front, Main and Second streets. The two most conspicuous were those of Mr. Valle, on Main street, built of Ste. Genevieve marble. Three hundred brick buildings were also in process of construction. The Glasgow Row, between Locust and St. Charles streets, and the houses of Messrs. Lucas and Gamble were most noteworthy, being in front of the Planters' House. The rapid growth of the city had increased the number of mechanics so much that they were induced to make a trial of their political strength

as a workingmen's party, and therefore selected Mr. John
M. Wimer as a candidate for the office of Mayor at the municipal election of that year, over a veteran competitor who
had held the office with great credit to himself several years
before. During this exciting canvass the progress of business was active. The Glasgow House was opened on the
2d of March, by Messrs. Wiley & Scollay, under the most flattering auspices, at the corner of Olive and Second streets, where,
under another name, it still flourishes. On the following day
the celebrated naturalist, John J. Audubon, arrived at the
house, accompanied by Edward Harris, Esq., of New Jersey,
on a quadrupedal and ornithological trip of collections and
observations for his celebrated book—the crown of all his
labors. The American Fur Company furnished him with every
facility for prosecuting his journey to the latitude of 47 degrees
and 20 minutes north—five miles above Fort Union and three
miles above the mouth of the Yellowstone river, where he
arrived on the 14th of June, 1843. There, under the auspices
of the company, he accomplished the task which had brought
him from Europe, and was returned with his friend to St. Louis
without cost or accident of any kind, and carried with him that
store of knowledge in quest of which he had traveled so far.
From St. Louis he proceeded with his friend to New York with
his rare and valuable collection, and from thence to France,
where, it is presumed, he completed the great labors which had
occupied his mind through the long period of his remarkable
life. St. Louis trappers, traders, boatmen, merchants, and all
those engaged in the explorations of the then distant wilds, had
joined in affording him every facility for accomplishing his
object, and it was said by those who accompanied him that
the Indians, and the children of the Upper Missouri Indians,
brought him rare birds and their eggs, and little quadrupeds, to
show their desire to add to the stock of knowledge which he
was accumulating.

The late city election had shown that St. Louis was still in
progress. She had elected a young mechanic, John M. Wimer,
Mayor, who was inaugurated on the 11th of April, and old
offices were now to be filled with younger incumbents of his
party. There was, however, none of that hasty action that

marks the age of folly in the proceedings of the City Council at that time, but considerate progress.

Mr. Joseph A. Wherry, who had succeeded his father as Register of the city, died a few days before the election. The father and the son had filled the same office for more than a quarter of a century with the regularity of the sun, and there is not to this day a better example of fidelity in office than those two gentlemen gave to the people of St. Louis.

There was no shock of credit, and German thalers and French five-francs were receivable and transferable during that active season with as much facility in commercial transactions as exchanges are made at Hamburg, Frankfort or London. In short, St. Louis had become the well-known center of the West, and its Briarean arms had been felt in the eastern hemisphere as in the United States. Wealthy emigrants crowded the steamboats bound for St. Louis from all parts of Europe. The whole taxable property in St. Louis was assessed at $11,721,425, and a levy of one per cent. made upon it as a city tax for that year.

Early in April the people of Jackson and Clay counties were thrown into great excitement by the arrival of ten persons from the western plains with large sums of specie, chiefly Mexican dollars, which they had robbed on the first of April from the merchant train of Antonio Jose Davi Chavis in the Indian country of the United States as he was traveling with his train of wagons on the road from Santa Fe to Independence to procure a stock of goods. After robbing him of his money they deliberately determined to murder him and drew lots for two to shoot him, which was done, the money divided and the party separated. On their arrival in detached parties they were apprehended by the citizens, who pursued them with commendable energy, recovered $7,500 of the money, and lodged them in the St. Louis jail. They were tried before the United States Court and punished. Two were hung near the Arsenal.

May 9th the Hon. Richard M. Johnson honored St. Louis with a formal visit and was received with all the formalities usual on such occasions; but truth compels us to state he was not believed to be the man who killed Tecumseh, so there was not that general enthusiasm manifested on the occasion that had been expected. However, the occasion was brilliant and passed off with eclat. A procession was formed and platforms and other accompaniments prepared for the occasion creditable to a city he had honored by a visit. The public were not disappointed in their distinguished visitor. He addressed them in that familiar, patriotic language which struck the heart and carried conviction with it that he was one of the American people who dared to do his duty. He was responded to in a suitable manner by a gentleman of taste and eloquence, and was escorted with suitable honors to his hotel, while the crowd lingered around the edifice to catch a view of the old Kentuckian who had either killed Tecumseh or led the lads who did it. Thus passed a patriot from the view of Missourians, but his example is with us and worthy of record and imitation. Colonel Johnson never said he killed Tecumseh.

Among the most enterprising and industrious of the fur traders and explorers of the regions of the Upper Missouri, in the most active days of that trade, when it formed the chief export of St. Louis and gave vitality to all commercial transactions, was Major Joshua Pilcher. He had received a liberal education, and studied physic for a profession; but, coming to St. Louis at a period of great activity in the fur trade, he was easily enticed into it, and became one of the most expert and efficient agents in the business and controlled the operations of one of the most successful companies that located their establishments on the Yellowstone river for near a quarter of a century.

He was a gentleman of the most kind and urbane disposition, and in all his traffic with the red men retained their confidence and friendship, and retired from their solitudes with their ardent wishes for his welfare when his age and strength admonished him to seek a more comfortable condition of life. Surrounded with all that affluence and kind friends could furnish, he ended his active life at the residence of General John Ruland on the the 5th of July, 1843, and was followed to his long resting place by some of the most devoted friends that it is possible for a long, active and virtuous life to throw about an individual. His memory will long be cherished by those whom he enriched by his industry and aided by his liberality and advice in the morning of life, when his example and experience were a rich treasure to all.

www.ingramcontent.com/pod-product-compliance
Lightning Source LLC
Chambersburg PA
CBHW022116160426
43197CB00009B/1054